D1389307

COOK'S KITCHEN

Grandma's Recipes

igloobooks

Published in 2014
by Igloo Books Ltd
Cottage Farm
Sywell
NN6 0BJ
www.igloobooks.com

Copyright © 2014 Igloo Books Ltd

All rights reserved. No part of this publication may be
reproduced or transmitted in any form or by any means,
electronic, or mechanical, including photocopying, recording,
or by any information storage and retrieval system,
without permission in writing from the publisher.
The measurements used are approximate.

Food photography and recipe development: PhotoCuisine UK
Front and back cover images © PhotoCuisine UK

OCE001 0714
2 4 6 8 10 9 7 5 3 1
ISBN 978-1-78343-530-2

Printed and manufactured in China

Contents

Snacks & Treats

Potato and Chorizo Hash

SERVES 2

PREPARATION TIME 25 MINUTES

COOKING TIME 20 MINUTES

INGREDIENTS

5 tbsp olive oil
1 red onion, quartered and sliced
1 red pepper, deseeded and cubed
150 g / 5 ½ oz / 1 cup chorizo, diced
200 g / 7 oz / 1 ⅓ cups boiled potatoes, cubed
1 tbsp thyme leaves
2 large eggs

METHOD

- Heat 4 tbsp of the oil in a large frying pan and fry the onion and pepper for 5 minutes to soften. Add the chorizo, potatoes and thyme and fry for 10 minutes, stirring only once every 2 minutes.

- Meanwhile, heat the rest of the oil in a separate frying pan and fry the eggs until the whites are set, but the yolks are still a little runny.

- Season the hash with salt and pepper then divide between 2 plates and top with the eggs.

TOP TIP
This recipe also works really well with leftover roast meat instead of the chorizo.

Tomato and Salami Tart

SERVES 6
PREPARATION TIME 10 MINUTES
COOKING TIME 20 MINUTES

INGREDIENTS

400 g / 14 oz ready-to-roll puff pastry
4 tbsp hummus
100 g / 3 ½ oz / ⅔ cup salami slices
3 medium tomatoes, sliced
4 black olives, pitted and sliced
a handful of rocket (arugula)

METHOD

- Preheat the oven to 220°C (200°C fan) / 425F / gas 7.

- Unroll the pastry into a rectangle on a lightly floured surface. Transfer the pastry to a non-stick baking tray.

- Spread the top of the pastry with hummus, leaving a 1 cm (½ in) border around the outside. Arrange the salami, tomatoes and olives on top.

- Transfer the baking tray to the oven and bake for 20 minutes or until the pastry is cooked through underneath. Scatter over the rocket and serve immediately.

TOP TIP
Replace the salami with prosciutto and the olives with capers.

Gammon and Salad Onion Skewers

SERVES 4
PREPARATION TIME 25 MINUTES
COOKING TIME 8 MINUTES

INGREDIENTS

6 salad onions

400 g / 14 oz / 2 cups unsmoked gammon, cubed

4 tbsp barbecue sauce

METHOD

- Put 12 wooden skewers in a bowl of water and leave to soak for 20 minutes.

- Meanwhile, cut off the green parts of the onions and reserve for garnish. Cut the bulb of each onion in half.

- Thread the gammon and onions onto the skewers and spread them out on a large grill tray.

- Brush them with barbecue sauce then grill for 4 minutes on each side or until the onions are slightly charred on the edges.

- Slice the reserved onion greens on the diagonal and scatter over the skewers.

TOP TIP

Add chunks of fresh pineapple to the skewers for a classic combination.

Stuffed Mussels

SERVES 4
PREPARATION TIME 15 MINUTES
COOKING TIME 10 MINUTES

INGREDIENTS

1.2 litres / 2 pints / 4 ¾ cups live mussels,
   scrubbed
100 g / 3 ½ oz / ½ cup butter, softened
2 cloves of garlic, crushed
3 tbsp flat leaf parsley, finely chopped
25 g / 1 oz / ⅓ cup breadcrumbs

METHOD

- Preheat the grill to its highest setting.

- Put a large saucepan over a high heat
  for 2 minutes. Tip in the mussels,
  put a lid on the pan and let them
  steam open in their own juices for
  5 minutes.

- When they have all opened, tip them
  out onto a baking tray. Remove and
  discard the empty side of the shells.

- Beat the butter with the garlic and
  parsley, then dot a little on top of each
  mussel. Sprinkle with breadcrumbs,
  then cook under the grill for
  3 minutes or until golden brown.

TOP TIP
Try this method
with oysters and
scallops too.

Baked Potato Wedges

SERVES 4

PREPARATION TIME 5 MINUTES

COOKING TIME 35–40 MINUTES

INGREDIENTS

4 tbsp olive oil

800 g / 1 lb 12 oz / 4 cups medium potatoes,
   cut into wedges

salt and pepper

METHOD

- Preheat the oven to 220°C (200°C fan) / 425F / gas 7.

- Put the oil in a large roasting tin and heat in the oven for 5 minutes.

- Carefully tip the potato wedges into the pan and turn to coat in the oil, then season well with salt and black pepper.

- Bake the wedges for 35–40 minutes, turning them every 15 minutes, until golden brown on the outside and fluffy within. Sprinkle with a little more sea salt and serve immediately.

TOP TIP
Finish the wedges with a few drops of truffle oil and a sprinkle of grated Parmesan.

Breadless Scotch Eggs

MAKES 6

PREPARATION TIME 15 MINUTES

COOKING TIME 25 MINUTES

INGREDIENTS

6 small eggs
6 good quality pork sausages
6 rashers streaky bacon

METHOD

- Preheat the oven to 180°C (160°C fan) / 350F / gas 4.

- Put the eggs in a pan of cold water then bring to a simmer and cook for 5 minutes. Plunge the eggs into cold water for 2 minutes then peel off the shells.

- Skin the sausages and divide the meat into 6. Flatten a portion of sausage meat onto your hand and put an egg in the centre, then squeeze the meat round the outside to coat. Repeat with the other 5 eggs.

- Wrap each egg in bacon then transfer to a roasting tin. Roast the Scotch eggs for 20 minutes or until the sausage meat is cooked through. Serve hot or cold.

TOP TIP
Try making this recipe with nduja instead of sausage meat for a spicy kick.

Tandoori Chicken Chapattis

SERVES 4
PREPARATION TIME 40 MINUTES
COOKING TIME 15 MINUTES

INGREDIENTS

1 lemon, juiced
3 tbsp tandoori spice mix
4 small skinless chicken breasts
¼ white cabbage, shredded
1 small red onion, quartered and thinly sliced
3 tbsp soured cream
1 lime, juiced
4 chapattis
coriander (cilantro) leaves to garnish
salt and pepper

METHOD

- Mix the lemon juice with the spice mix and a pinch of salt and rub it all over the chicken. Leave to marinate for 30 minutes.

- Mix the cabbage and onion with the soured cream and lime juice and season with salt and pepper.

- Preheat the grill to its highest setting.

- Grill the chicken breasts for 15 minutes, turning regularly, until cooked through and lightly charred in places.

- Fill the chapattis with the cabbage mixture. Slice the chicken breasts on the diagonal and transfer to the chapattis, then garnish with coriander and serve immediately.

TOP TIP
Serve the chapattis with mango chutney for dipping.

Orange and Passion Fruit Verrines

SERVES 4
PREPARATION TIME 20 MINUTES

INGREDIENTS

2 oranges

50 g / 1 ¾ oz / ½ cup icing (confectioners')
    sugar, sieved

450 g / 1 lb / 2 cups Greek yoghurt

4 passion fruit

150 g / 5 ½ oz / ⅔ cup coconut cake, cubed

METHOD

- Use a vegetable peeler to pare 4 thin slices of orange zest and reserve for decoration. Slice the top and bottom off the oranges. Slice away the peel then cut out each individual segment, leaving the white pith behind. Discard the pith.

- Fold the icing sugar into the yoghurt.

- Divide the orange segments between 4 glass bowls and top with the pulp and seeds from 2 of the passion fruit. Spoon over half of the yoghurt.

- Arrange the cake cubes on top, then spoon over the rest of the yoghurt and top with the rest of the passion fruit pulp. Garnish with the reserved orange zest.

TOP TIP
Try using ruby grapefruit for a sharper flavour.

Lemon Syrup Cake

SERVES 8

PREPARATION TIME 15 MINUTES

COOKING TIME 40 MINUTES

SOAKING TIME 20 MINUTES

INGREDIENTS

175 g / 6 oz / 1 ¼ cups self-raising flour, sifted

1 tsp baking powder

175 g / 6 oz / ¾ cup caster (superfine) sugar

175 g / 6 oz / ¾ cup butter, softened

3 large eggs

2 lemons, zest finely grated

FOR THE SOAKING SYRUP

2 lemons, zest finely pared

100 ml / 3 ½ fl. oz / ½ cup lemon juice

100 g / 3 ½ oz / ½ cup caster (superfine) sugar

METHOD

- Preheat the oven to 180°C (160°C fan) / 350F / gas 4 and oil and line a 23 cm (9 in) round cake tin with greaseproof paper.

- Combine the flour, baking powder, sugar, butter, eggs and lemon zest in a bowl and whisk together for 2 minutes or until smooth.

- Scrape the mixture into the tin and level the top then bake for 40 minutes or until a toothpick inserted in the centre comes out clean.

- Put the lemon zest, lemon juice and caster sugar in a small saucepan and stir over a low heat until the sugar dissolves. Increase the heat and simmer without stirring for 3 minutes or until the lemon zest has softened and the syrup has thickened a little.

- Pour the syrup over the hot cake then leave to soak and cool in its tin for 20 minutes. Transfer the cake to a wire rack and leave to cool completely before slicing and serving.

TOP TIP

Make a quick icing by stirring a little lemon juice into sieved icing sugar.

Blueberry and Almond Tray Bake

SERVES 10

PREPARATION TIME 15 MINUTES

COOKING TIME 30 MINUTES

INGREDIENTS

200 g / 7 oz / 1 ⅓ cups self-raising flour, sifted

50 g / 1 ¾ oz / ½ cup ground almonds

175 g / 6 oz / ¾ cup caster (superfine) sugar

175 g / 6 oz / ¾ cup butter, softened

3 large eggs

1 lemon, zest finely grated

100 g / 3 ½ oz / ⅔ cup blueberries

50 g / 1 ¾ oz / ⅔ cup flaked (slivered) almonds

2 tbsp granulated sugar

1 tsp ground cinnamon

METHOD

- Preheat the oven to 160°C (140°C fan) / 325F / gas 3 and line a 15 cm x 25 cm (6 in x 10 in) baking tin with greaseproof paper.

- Combine the flour, ground almonds, caster sugar, butter, eggs and lemon zest in a bowl and whisk together for 2 minutes or until smooth. Fold in the blueberries then scrape the mixture into the tin and level the top.

- Sprinkle over the flaked almonds then bake for 30 minutes or until a toothpick inserted in the centre comes out clean.

- Transfer to a wire rack and leave to cool completely. Mix the granulated sugar with the cinnamon and sprinkle it over the cake, then cut into 10 pieces.

TOP TIP

This recipe also works well with stoned cherries in place of the blueberries.

Mini Paris Brest

MAKES 6
PREPARATION TIME 45 MINUTES
COOKING TIME 20 MINUTES

INGREDIENTS

55 g / 2 oz / ¼ cup butter, cubed
70 g / 2 ½ oz / ½ cup strong white bread
    flour, sieved
2 large eggs, beaten
50 g / 2 ½ oz / ⅔ cup flaked (slivered)
    almonds
225 ml / 8 fl. oz double (heavy) cream
4 tbsp hazelnut (cob nut) syrup
icing (confectioners') sugar to dust

METHOD

- Preheat the oven to 200°C (180°C fan) / 400F / gas 6.

- Oil and line a large baking tray with greaseproof paper, then spray it with water.

- Bring the butter and 150 ml / ¼ pint / ⅔ cup cold water to the boil then beat in the flour off the heat. Continue to beat until you have a smooth ball of pastry that leaves the sides of the saucepan clean. Stir in the beaten egg a little at a time to make a glossy paste.

- Spoon the pastry into a piping bag fitted with a large star nozzle and pipe 6 rings onto the prepared baking tray.

- Sprinkle with almonds and bake for 20 minutes, increasing the heat to 220°C (200°C fan) / 425F / gas 7 halfway through.

- Transfer the choux rings to a wire rack, cut in half horizontally and leave to cool completely.

- Whip the cream with the hazelnut syrup until thick then spoon into a piping bag fitted with a large star nozzle. Sandwich the choux rings back together with the hazelnut cream, then dust liberally with icing sugar.

TOP TIP
Try adding 2 tbsp of Frangelico liqueur to the cream.

Viennese Shortbread

MAKES 24
PREPARATION TIME 10 MINUTES
COOKING TIME 15–20 MINUTES

INGREDIENTS

175 g / 6 oz / ¾ cup butter, softened
50 g / 1 ¾ oz / ¼ cup caster (superfine) sugar
½ tsp vanilla extract
175 g / 6 oz / 1 ¼ cups self-raising flour

METHOD

- Preheat the oven to 170°C (150°C fan) / 340F / gas 3 and line 2 baking trays with non-stick baking paper.

- Cream the butter, sugar and vanilla extract together with an electric whisk until pale and well whipped then stir in the flour.

- Spoon the mixture into a piping bag fitted with a large star nozzle and pipe 12 rosettes onto each tray.

- Bake the biscuits for 15–20 minutes or until they are lightly golden.

- Transfer the biscuits to a wire rack and leave to cool completely before serving.

TOP TIP
Try sandwiching the biscuits together with buttercream and jam.

Coconut Jam Biscuits

MAKES 12

PREPARATION TIME 30 MINUTES

COOKING TIME 12 MINUTES

INGREDIENTS

2 large egg whites

100 g / 3 ½ oz / ½ cup caster (superfine) sugar

250 g / 9 oz / 1 ¼ cups desiccated coconut

4 tbsp strawberry jam (jelly)

METHOD

- Preheat the oven to 170°C (150°C fan) / 325F / gas 3 and line a baking tray with greaseproof paper.

- Whisk the egg whites to stiff peaks in a very clean bowl then carefully fold in the sugar and coconut.

- Spoon the mixture into a piping bag fitted with a large star nozzle and pipe 12 circles onto the prepared baking tray. Bake the biscuits for 12 minutes or until they start to turn golden on top.

- Transfer to a wire rack and leave to cool completely before spooning a little jam into the centre of each one.

TOP TIP

Replace the jam with chocolate hazelnut (cob nut) spread.

Easy Strawberry Sorbet

MAKES 500 ml

PREPARATION TIME 15 MINUTES

FREEZING TIME 2 HOURS 30 MINUTES

INGREDIENTS

400 g / 14 oz / 2 ⅔ cups strawberries, sliced

50 g / 1 ¾ oz / ½ cup icing (confectioners') sugar

1 egg white, lightly beaten

ice cream cones to serve

METHOD

- Freeze the sliced strawberries for 2 hours.

- Transfer the frozen fruit to a food processor with the icing sugar and blend until smooth. Add the egg white and blend again, then scrape the mixture into a plastic tub and freeze for 30 minutes or until firm.

- Scoop the sorbet into ice cream cones to serve.

TOP TIP
This sorbet recipe works with any frozen berries.

Lemon Meringue Pies

MAKES 6

PREPARATION TIME 1 HOUR

COOKING TIME 30 MINUTES

INGREDIENTS

100 g / 3 ½ oz / ½ cup butter, cubed

200 g / 7 oz / 1 ⅓ cups plain (all purpose) flour

225 g / 8 oz / 1 cup lemon curd

4 large egg whites

110 g / 4 oz / ½ cup caster (superfine) sugar

METHOD

- Preheat the oven to 200°C (180°C fan) / 400F / gas 6.

- Rub the butter into the flour and add just enough cold water to bind. Chill for 30 minutes then roll out on a floured surface and cut out 6 circles with a large round cookie cutter. Use the pastry circles to line a 6-hole deep muffin tin and prick the bases with a fork.

- Line the pastry with cling film and fill with baking beans or rice then bake for 10 minutes. Remove the cling film and beans and cook for another 8 minutes to crisp. Fill the pastry cases with lemon curd.

- Whisk the egg whites until stiff, then gradually add the sugar and whisk until the mixture is thick and shiny. Spoon the meringue into a piping bag fitted with a large star nozzle and pipe a swirl on top of each pie. Return the tin to the oven to bake for 10 minutes or until golden brown. Serve hot or cold.

TOP TIP

Try using passion fruit curd instead of lemon curd.

Marmalade Gateau Breton

SERVES 6
PREPARATION TIME 15 MINUTES
COOKING TIME 40–45 MINUTES

INGREDIENTS

250 g / 9 oz / 1 ¼ cups butter, cubed
250 g / 9 oz / 1 ⅔ cups plain (all purpose) flour
250 g / 9 oz / 1 ¼ cups caster (superfine) sugar
5 large egg yolks
175 g / 6 oz / ½ cup marmalade
icing (confectioners') sugar for dusting
salt

METHOD

- Preheat the oven to 180°C (160°C fan) / 350F / gas 4 and butter a 20 cm (8 in) round loose-bottomed cake tin.

- Rub the butter into the flour with a pinch of salt then stir in the sugar.

- Beat the egg yolks and stir them into the dry ingredients.

- Bring the mixture together into a soft dough and divide it in two. Put 1 half in the freezer for 10 minutes. Press the other half into the bottom of the cake tin to form an even layer. Spread the marmalade on top.

- Coarsely grate the other half of the dough over the top and press down lightly.

- Bake the gateau for 40–45 minutes or until golden brown and cooked through.

- Cool completely before unmoulding and dust with icing sugar.

TOP TIP
This recipe also works well with jam in place of the marmalade.

Jam Sandwich Biscuits

MAKES 36

PREPARATION TIME 1 HOUR 15 MINUTES

COOKING TIME 25 MINUTES

INGREDIENTS

150 g / 5 ½ oz / ⅔ cup caster (superfine) sugar

350 g / 12 oz / 1 ½ cups butter, softened

1 lemon, zest finely grated

300 g / 10 ½ oz / 2 cups plain (all purpose) flour

150 g / 5 ½ oz / 1 ½ cups ground almonds

250 g / 9 oz / 1 cup plum jam (jelly)

icing (confectioners') sugar for dusting

METHOD

- Cream together the sugar, butter and lemon zest until pale and well whipped then stir in the flour and ground almonds. Bring the mixture together into a ball with your hands then wrap in cling film and refrigerate for 45 minutes.

- Preheat the oven to 140°C (120°C fan) / 275F / gas 1 and line 2 baking sheets with greaseproof paper.

- Roll out the dough on a lightly floured surface to 5 mm thick. Use an oval fluted pastry cutter to cut out 72 biscuits, rerolling the trimmings as necessary. Use a small round cutter to cut 2 holes out of the centre of 36 of the biscuits.

- Transfer the biscuits to the prepared trays and bake in batches for 25 minutes or until cooked through and golden.

- Transfer the biscuits to a wire rack and leave to cool completely.

- Sandwich the plain biscuits and centre-less biscuits together in pairs with the jam then dust lightly with icing sugar.

TOP TIP

Try replacing the jam with marmalade.

Linseed Rock Cakes

MAKES 16

PREPARATION TIME 10 MINUTES

COOKING TIME 15 MINUTES

INGREDIENTS

100 g / 3 ½ oz / ½ cup butter

200 g / 7 oz / 1 ⅓ cups wholemeal self-raising
    flour

100 g / 3 ½ oz / ½ cup caster (superfine) sugar

100 g / 3 ½ oz / ½ cup almonds, finely
    chopped

4 tbsp linseeds

1 large egg

2 tbsp milk

METHOD

- Preheat the oven to 200°C (180°C fan) / 390F / gas 6 and grease a large baking tray.

- Rub the butter into the flour until the mixture resembles fine breadcrumbs then stir in the sugar, almonds and linseeds.

- Beat the egg with the milk and stir it into the dry ingredients to make a sticky dough.

- Use a dessert spoon to portion the mixture onto the baking tray, leaving the surface quite rough.

- Bake the rock cakes for 15 minutes then transfer them to a wire rack and leave to cool.

TOP TIP

The linseeds can be replaced with poppy seeds or sesame seeds.

Peanut Millionaire's Shortbread

MAKES **6**

PREPARATION TIME **20 MINUTES**

COOKING TIME **3 HOURS 20 MINUTES**

CHILLING TIME **2 HOURS**

INGREDIENTS

400 g / 14 oz / 1 ⅔ cups can of condensed milk

150 g / 5 ½ oz / 1 cup salted peanuts

200 g / 7 oz / 1 cup dark chocolate (minimum 70% cocoa solids), chopped

50 g / 1 ¾ oz / ¼ cup butter

FOR THE SHORTBREAD

225 g / 8 oz / 1 ½ cups plain (all purpose) flour

75 g / 2 ½ oz / ⅓ cup caster (superfine) sugar

150 g / 5 oz / ⅔ cup butter, cubed

METHOD

- Make the caramel layer in advance. Put the unopened can of condensed milk in a saucepan of water and simmer for 3 hours, adding more water as necessary to ensure it doesn't boil dry. Leave the can to cool completely.

- Preheat the oven to 180°C (160°C fan) / 350F / gas 4 and line a 20 cm (8 in) square cake tin with greaseproof paper.

- To make the shortbread, mix together the flour and sugar in a bowl, then rub in the butter.

- Knead gently until the mixture forms a smooth dough then press it into the bottom of the tin in an even layer.

- Bake the shortbread for 20 minutes, turning the tray round halfway through. Leave to cool.

- Open the can of condensed milk and beat the caramel until smooth. Fold in the peanuts then spread it over the shortbread and chill for 1 hour.

- Put the chocolate and butter in a bowl set over a pan of simmering water and stir together until melted and smooth.

- Pour the mixture over the caramel layer and leave to cool and set before cutting into 6 bars.

TOP TIP

Drizzle some white chocolate over the top of the shortbread.

Individual Apple Puff Pies

MAKES 12

PREPARATION TIME 30 MINUTES

COOKING TIME 20 MINUTES

INGREDIENTS

2 large Bramley apples, peeled, cored and chopped

4 tbsp caster (superfine) sugar

½ tsp freshly grated nutmeg

900 g / 2 lb / 3 cups ready-to-roll puff pastry

icing (confectioners') sugar for dusting

METHOD

- Preheat the oven to 220°C (200°C fan) / 425F / gas 7.

- Put the apples and sugar in a saucepan with 2 tbsp of water. Cover the pan and cook over a medium heat for 10 minutes, stirring occasionally. Leave to cool then stir in the nutmeg.

- Roll out the pastry on a lightly floured surface and cut out 12 large circles and 12 smaller circles. Use the large circles to line a 12-hole deep muffin tin. Fill the pastry with the apple mixture, then top with the smaller pastry circles.

- Bake the pies for 20 minutes or until the tops are golden and the bottoms are crisp. Serve warm or cold, dusted with plenty of icing sugar.

TOP TIP

Stir a handful of sultanas through the apple mixture before filling the pies.

Scones with Yoghurt and Jam

MAKES 12

PREPARATION TIME 25 MINUTES

COOKING TIME 15 MINUTES

INGREDIENTS

225 g / 8 oz / 1 ½ cups self-raising flour

55 g / 2 oz / ¼ cup butter

150 ml / 5 fl. oz / ⅔ cup milk

200 g / 7 oz / ¾ cup strawberry jam (jelly)

200 g / 7 oz / ¾ cup strawberry flavoured
    Greek yoghurt

METHOD

- Preheat the oven to 220°C (200°C fan) / 425F / gas 7 and oil a large baking sheet.

- Sieve the flour into a bowl and rub in the butter until the mixture resembles fine breadcrumbs. Stir in enough milk to bring the mixture together into a soft dough.

- Flatten the dough with your hands on a floured work surface until 2.5 cm (1 in) thick. Use a pastry cutter to cut out 12 circles and transfer them to the prepared baking sheet.

- Bake in the oven for 15 minutes or until golden brown and cooked through. Transfer the scones to a wire rack to cool completely

- Cut each scone in half and top with jam and yoghurt.

TOP TIP
For a more decadent treat, replace the yoghurt with clotted cream.

Pancakes with Fruit Salad

SERVES 4
PREPARATION TIME 15 MINUTES
COOKING TIME 25 MINUTES

INGREDIENTS

250 g / 9 oz / 1 ⅔ cups plain (all purpose) flour
2 tsp baking powder
4 large eggs
300 ml / 10 ½ fl. oz / 1 ¼ cups milk
2 tbsp butter
icing (confectioners') sugar for dusting
4 tbsp runny honey

FOR THE FRUIT SALAD

1 mango, peeled, stoned and sliced
150 g / 5 ½ oz / 1 cup strawberries, quartered
2 bananas, sliced
1 tbsp mint leaves, shredded
3 tbsp lemon curd

METHOD

- Mix the flour and baking powder in a bowl and make a well in the centre. Break in 2 of the eggs and pour in the milk then use a whisk to gradually incorporate all of the flour from round the outside.

- Melt the butter in a frying pan then whisk it into the batter. Put the buttered frying pan back over a low heat. You will need a tablespoon of batter for each pancake and you should be able to cook 4 pancakes at a time in the frying pan.

- Spoon the batter into the pan and cook for 2 minutes or until small bubbles start to appear on the surface. Turn the pancakes over with a spatula and cook the other side until golden brown and cooked through.

- Repeat until all the batter has been used, keeping the finished batches warm in a low oven.

- Toss together the mango, strawberries, banana and mint and arrange on a serving platter. Pile the pancakes next to the fruit and dust them with icing sugar before drizzling with honey. Spoon the lemon curd over the fruit and serve immediately.

TOP TIP
This fruit salad is also delicious served with waffles.

Pain d'Epice

SERVES 8
PREPARATION TIME 15 MINUTES
COOKING TIME 40 MINUTES

INGREDIENTS

250 g / 9 oz / 1 ⅔ cups self-raising flour
2 tsp ground ginger
1 tsp mixed spice
200 g / 8 ½ oz / ⅔ cup golden syrup
125 g / 4 ½ oz / ½ cup butter
125 g / 4 ½ oz / ¾ cup light brown sugar
2 large eggs, beaten
250 ml / 9 fl. oz / 1 cup milk
3 tbsp sugar nibs

METHOD

- Preheat the oven to 180°C (160°C fan) / 355F / gas 4 and grease and line a loaf tin.

- Sieve the flour and spices into a bowl.

- Put the golden syrup, butter and brown sugar in a small saucepan and boil gently for 2 minutes, stirring to dissolve the sugar. Add the butter and sugar mixture to the flour with the eggs and milk and fold it all together until smooth.

- Scrape the mixture into the prepared tin and sprinkle with sugar nibs then bake for 40 minutes. The cake is ready when a skewer inserted in the centre comes out clean. Transfer the cake to a wire rack and leave to cool completely before slicing.

TOP TIP
This cake will keep for up to 1 week if stored in an airtight tin.

Profiteroles

MAKES 24
PREPARATION TIME 45 MINUTES
COOKING TIME 20 MINUTES

INGREDIENTS

55 g / 2 oz / ¼ cup butter, cubed
75 g / 2 ½ oz / ½ cup strong white bread flour,
    sieved
2 large eggs, beaten
225 ml / 8 fl. oz / 1 cup double (heavy) cream
100 g / 3 ½ oz / 1 cup icing (confectioners')
    sugar
100 ml / 3 ½ fl. oz / ½ cup chocolate sauce
2 tbsp white chocolate sprinkles

METHOD

- Preheat the oven to 200°C (180°C fan) / 400F / gas 6. Line a baking tray with greaseproof paper and spray with a little water.

- Melt the butter with 150 ml / ¼ pint / ⅓ cup water and bring to the boil. Immediately beat in the flour, off the heat, with a wooden spoon until it forms a smooth ball of pastry. Incorporate the egg a little at a time to make a glossy paste.

- Spoon the pastry into a piping bag fitted with a large plain nozzle and pipe 2.5 cm (1 in) buns onto the baking tray.

- Bake for 20 minutes, increasing the temperature to 220°C (200°C fan) / 425F / gas 7 halfway through. Transfer the choux buns to a wire rack and make a hole in the underneath of each one so the steam can escape. Leave to cool completely.

- Whip the cream until thick, then spoon it into a piping bag and fill the choux buns through the steam hole.

- Stir a few drops of water into the icing sugar until you get a pourable icing then drizzle it over the profiteroles. Squeeze over the chocolate sauce then decorate with white chocolate sprinkles.

TOP TIP
Don't make the choux buns too large, as they may not cook through.

Homemade Meals

Spanish Chicken

SERVES 4

PREPARATION TIME 10 MINUTES

COOKING TIME 50 MINUTES

INGREDIENTS

3 tbsp olive oil

4 chicken quarters

450 g / 1 lb / 2 cups baby new potatoes

8 shallots, peeled

2 red peppers, deseeded and cut into wedges

1 bulb of garlic, separated into cloves

2 tbsp flat leaf parsley, chopped

salt and black pepper

METHOD

- Preheat the oven to 200°C (180°C fan) / 400F / gas 6.

- Heat the oil in a large roasting tin on the hob. Season the chicken with salt and pepper, then sear the skin in the oil.

- Stir in the potatoes, shallots, peppers and garlic, making sure everything is coated with the oil, then season with salt and pepper.

- Transfer the tin to the oven and roast for 50 minutes, stirring half way through. To check if the chicken is cooked, pierce the thickest part of a thigh with a skewer. If the juices run clear it's ready. Serve hot, sprinkled with parsley.

TOP TIP
Try strips of pork belly in place of the chicken.

58

Carrot and Pine Nut Soup

SERVES 6
PREPARATION TIME 10 MINUTES
COOKING TIME 25 MINUTES

INGREDIENTS

2 tbsp olive oil
2 tbsp butter
1 onion, finely chopped
2 cloves of garlic, crushed
4 carrots, diced
1 litre / 1 pint 15 fl. oz / 4 cups vegetable stock
4 tbsp double (heavy) cream
4 tbsp extra virgin olive oil
2 tbsp pine nuts
salt and black pepper

METHOD

- Heat the oil and butter in a saucepan and fry the onion for 5 minutes or until softened.

- Add the garlic and carrots to the pan and cook for 2 more minutes, then stir in the stock and bring to the boil.

- Simmer for 15 minutes or until the carrots are tender. Ladle the soup into a liquidiser and blend until smooth then season to taste with salt and pepper.

- Divide the soup between 6 warm mugs. Add a drizzle of cream and oil to the top of each, then sprinkle with pine nuts and serve immediately.

TOP TIP
This recipe also works well with parsnips instead of the carrots.

Cod with Stewed Leeks and Peppers

SERVES 4

PREPARATION TIME 5 MINUTES

COOKING TIME 20 MINUTES

INGREDIENTS

2 tbsp butter

3 leeks, sliced

175 ml / 6 fl. oz / ⅔ cup dry white wine

4 tbsp olive oil

4 portions cod fillet

1 onion, sliced

3 red peppers, deseeded and cubed

1 tsp smoked paprika

2 tsp caster (superfine) sugar

2 tbsp sherry vinegar

flat leaf parsley to garnish

METHOD

- Preheat the oven to 180°C (160°C fan) / 350F / gas 4.

- Heat the butter in an ovenproof frying pan then gently fry the leeks for 5 minutes without colouring. Turn up the heat and pour in the wine, then simmer for 2 minutes.

- Heat half of the oil in a separate frying pan and sear the skin-side of the cod portions. Transfer them to the top of the leeks, skin side up, then put the pan in the oven and roast for 10 minutes.

- Meanwhile, heat the rest of the oil in the cod pan and fry the onion and peppers for 8 minutes. Sprinkle over the paprika then stir in the sugar and vinegar and simmer for 2 minutes.

- Serve the cod on a bed of leeks with the peppers on the side. Garnish with parsley.

TOP TIP
This recipe tastes delicious with any white fish – try pollock or haddock.

Chicken and Vegetable Chorba

SERVES 4
PREPARATION TIME 5 MINUTES
COOKING TIME 15 MINUTES

INGREDIENTS

1.2 litres / 2 pints / 4 ¾ cups chicken stock
1 potato, peeled and diced
1 carrot, peeled and chopped
100 g / 3 ½ oz / 1 cup dried vermicelli
1 courgette (zucchini), diced
1 leek, chopped
225 g / 8 oz / 1 cup chicken breast, cubed
½ tsp ground cumin
½ tsp ground ginger
coriander (cilantro) leaves to garnish
salt and black pepper

METHOD

- Bring the stock to the boil then add the potatoes and carrots and cook for 8 minutes. Add the vermicelli, leek and courgette to the pan and cook for 4 minutes.

- Stir the chicken, cumin and ginger into the soup and simmer gently for 3 minutes or until the chicken is just cooked through.

- Taste the soup and adjust the seasoning with salt and pepper. Ladle into 4 warm bowls and garnish with coriander.

TOP TIP
Try serving the chorba with coriander flatbreads.

Lasagne

SERVES 6
PREPARATION TIME 15 MINUTES
COOKING TIME 1 HOUR 30 MINUTES

INGREDIENTS

4 tbsp olive oil
1 onion, finely chopped
1 carrot, finely chopped
1 celery stick, finely chopped
3 cloves of garlic, crushed
450 g / 1 lb / 2 cups minced beef
400 g / 14 oz / 2 cups canned tomatoes,
    chopped
1 beef stock cube
2 tbsp butter
2 tbsp plain (all purpose) flour
600 ml / 1 pint / 2 ½ cups whole milk
400 g / 14 oz / 2 cups dried lasagne sheets
4 tbsp Parmesan, finely grated
salt and black pepper

METHOD

- Preheat the oven to 200°C (180°C fan) / 400F / gas 6.

- Heat the oil in a sauté pan and fry the onion, carrot and celery for 10 minutes or until softened. Add the garlic and cook for 2 more minutes. Add the mince and stir-fry until browned.

- Add the chopped tomatoes and stock cube and bring to a simmer, then cook over a low heat for 30 minutes.

- Meanwhile, melt the butter in a small saucepan. Stir in the flour then gradually incorporate the milk, stirring continuously to avoid any lumps forming. Simmer the sauce until it thickens, then season to taste with salt and pepper.

- Starting with a layer of lasagne sheets, layer up the meat sauce, white sauce and pasta until everything has been used, finishing with a layer of white sauce.

- Sprinkle the top with Parmesan, then bake the lasagne for 45 minutes or until the top is golden brown and the pasta is tender all the way through.

TOP TIP

Top the lasagne with slices of mozzarella before sprinkling with Parmesan.

Bresaola and Barley Soup

SERVES 4
PREPARATION TIME 5 MINUTES
COOKING TIME 50 MINUTES

INGREDIENTS

2 tbsp olive oil
1 leek, sliced
1 carrot, diced
½ celery stick, diced
150 g / 5 ½ oz / ¾ cup pearl barley
1 litre / 1 pint 15 fl. oz / 4 cups beef stock
8 slices bresaola, cut into thick strips
1 tbsp chives, chopped
salt and black pepper

METHOD

- Heat the oil in a large saucepan and gently fry the leek, carrot and celery for 5 minutes without colouring. Stir in the stock and bring to the boil.

- Turn the heat down and simmer the soup for 45 minutes or until the barley is tender. Season to taste with salt and pepper.

- Ladle the soup into 4 warm bowls and top with the bresaola and chives.

TOP TIP
You can easily substitute the bresaola with prosciutto.

Barbecue Baby Back Ribs

SERVES 4

PREPARATION TIME 4 HOURS 30 MINUTES

COOKING TIME 3 HOURS

INGREDIENTS

2 tbsp olive oil

1 small onion, grated

3 cloves of garlic, crushed

1 tbsp fresh ginger, finely grated

1 tsp mixed spice

200 ml / 7 fl. oz / ¾ cup tomato passata

200 ml / 7 fl. oz / ¾ cup apple juice

3 tbsp dark brown sugar

1 ½ lemons, juiced

1 tbsp Worcestershire sauce

1 tbsp Dijon mustard

2 racks of baby back pork ribs,
    membrane removed

salt

METHOD

- Heat the oil in a saucepan and fry the onion, garlic and ginger for 3 minutes without colouring. Stir in the mixed spice then add the passata, apple juice, sugar, lemon juice, Worcestershire sauce and mustard with a large pinch of salt and bring to the boil.

- Turn down the heat and simmer for 10 minutes or until the sauce is thick and smooth.

- Leave the sauce to cool, then brush half of it over the ribs and leave to marinate in the fridge for 4 hours or overnight.

- Preheat the oven to 110°C (90°C fan) / 225F / gas ¼.

- Transfer the ribs to a roasting tin and slow-roast for 3 hours, turning occasionally and basting with the rest of the sauce.

- The ribs can either be served straight away or cooked over a hot charcoal barbecue for a few minutes to give a smoky taste.

TOP TIP

This marinade also works well with beef shortribs.

Mustard-roasted Collar Bacon

SERVES 8

PREPARATION TIME 25 MINUTES

COOKING TIME 2 HOURS 20 MINUTES

INGREDIENTS

3 kg / 6 lb 8 oz piece collar bacon or gammon

2 carrots, cut into large chunks

2 celery sticks, cut into large chunks

2 onions, cut into large chunks

1 tbsp black peppercorns

2 bay leaves

3 tbsp Dijon mustard

3 tbsp grain mustard

4 cloves of garlic, unpeeled

a small bunch of thyme

METHOD

- Put the collar bacon in a saucepan of cold water. Bring to the boil then discard the water.

- Add the vegetables to the pan with enough cold water to cover the meat by 5 cm (2 in). Bring to a gentle simmer and skim any scum off the surface.

- Add the peppercorns and bay leaves, then put on a lid and simmer gently for 2 hours.

- Remove the bacon from the saucepan and leave to steam dry in a baking dish for 5 minutes.

- Preheat the oven to 220°C (200°C fan) / 425F / gas 7.

- Mix the 2 mustards together and slather it over the collar bacon. Add the garlic cloves to the dish and sprinkle the thyme over the top.

- Transfer the bacon to the oven and roast for 20 minutes. Serve hot or leave to cool completely before slicing and serving cold.

TOP TIP
Try replacing the mustard with horseradish sauce.

Winter Minestrone

SERVES 6
PREPARATION TIME 5 MINUTES
COOKING TIME 20 MINUTES

INGREDIENTS

2 tbsp olive oil

1 onion, finely chopped

1 carrot, diced

1 celery stick, diced

1 tbsp rosemary, chopped

2 cloves of garlic, finely chopped

2 rashers streaky bacon, chopped

1.2 litres / 2 pints / 4 ¾ cups vegetable stock

150 g / 5 ½ oz / 1 ½ cups dried ditalini or
    similar pasta shapes

400 g / 14 oz / 2 cups canned tomatoes,
    chopped

3 tbsp Parmesan, grated

METHOD

- Heat the oil in a large saucepan and fry the onion, carrot and celery for 5 minutes without colouring. Add the rosemary, garlic and bacon and fry for 2 more minutes.

- Pour in the stock and bring to the boil, then add the pasta and cook for 10 minutes or until al dente.

- Stir in the canned tomatoes and return to the boil, then ladle into warm bowls and sprinkle with Parmesan.

TOP TIP
Try stirring a little pesto into each bowl for greater depth of flavour.

Spring Vegetable Minestrone

SERVES 4
PREPARATION TIME 5 MINUTES
COOKING TIME 15 MINUTES

INGREDIENTS

1.2 litres / 2 pints / 4 ¾ cups vegetable stock
100 g / 3 ½ oz / 1 cup dried spaccatelle or
    similar pasta shapes
12 asparagus spears, cut into short lengths
1 courgette (zucchini), sliced
4 spring onions (scallions), chopped
2 medium tomatoes, peeled and chopped
3 tbsp pesto
50 g / ¾ oz / ½ cup piece of Parmesan

METHOD

- Bring the vegetable stock to the boil then cook the pasta for 5 minutes.

- Add the asparagus and courgette slices to the pan, bring it back to the boil then simmer for a further 5 minutes.

- Add the spring onions and tomatoes and simmer until the pasta and asparagus are just al dente.

- Stir in the pesto then ladle the soup into 4 warm bowls. Use a vegetable peeler to shave the Parmesan over the minestrone and serve straight away.

TOP TIP
Try poaching cubes of salmon in the soup for a few minutes.

Pea and Asparagus Lasagne

SERVES 6

PREPARATION TIME 15 MINUTES

COOKING TIME 1 HOUR

INGREDIENTS

2 tbsp butter

2 cloves of garlic, crushed

2 tbsp plain (all purpose) flour

600 ml / 1 pint / 2 ½ cups vegetable stock

100 ml / 3 ½ fl. oz / ½ cup double (heavy) cream

12 asparagus spears, cut into short lengths

200 g / 7 oz / 1 ⅓ cups frozen peas, defrosted

2 tbsp flat leaf parsley, finely chopped

1 tbsp mint leaves, finely chopped

1 tbsp thyme leaves

400 g / 14 oz / 2 cups dried lasagne sheets

4 tbsp Parmesan, finely grated

salt and black pepper

METHOD

- Preheat the oven to 200°C (180°C fan) / 400F / gas 6.

- Melt the butter in a small saucepan and fry the garlic for 30 seconds. Stir in the flour then gradually incorporate the stock and cream, stirring continuously to avoid any lumps forming.

- Simmer the sauce until it thickens, then season to taste with salt and pepper. Set aside a ladle of the sauce, then stir the asparagus, peas and herbs into the rest and simmer for 2 more minutes.

- Layer up the lasagne sheets with the vegetables in a greased baking dish, finishing with a layer of lasagne.

- Pour the reserved sauce over the top and sprinkle with Parmesan, then bake the lasagne for 45 minutes or until the top is golden brown and the pasta is tender all the way through.

TOP TIP

Swap the asparagus for purple sprouting broccoli when not in season.

Mussel Soup

SERVES 6

PREPARATION TIME 5 MINUTES

COOKING TIME 12 MINUTES

INGREDIENTS

2 tbsp olive oil

1 leek, sliced

2 cloves of garlic, sliced

1.2 litres / 2 pints / 4 ¾ cups fish stock

1.2 litres / 2 pints / 4 ¾ cups live mussels,
    scrubbed

2 medium tomatoes, peeled and chopped

1 tbsp flat leaf parsley, chopped

salt and black pepper

METHOD

- Heat the oil in a large saucepan and
  fry the leek and garlic for 4 minutes
  without colouring. Pour in the fish
  stock and bring to a simmer, then
  add the mussels and put on a lid.

- Simmer for 5 minutes or until all the
  shells have opened, then stir in the
  tomatoes and warm through. Season
  to taste with salt and pepper.

- Ladle into hot bowls and garnish
  with parsley.

TOP TIP

This soup also works
really well with clams
or cockles.

Spice-crusted Lamb Salad

SERVES 4

PREPARATION TIME 10 MINUTES

COOKING TIME 15 MINUTES

INGREDIENTS

4 x 4-bone racks of lamb, French trimmed

3 tbsp tahini paste

2 tbsp ras el hanout spice mix

200 g / 7 oz / 1 cup canned chickpeas, drained

150 g / 5 ½ oz / 1 cup cherry tomatoes, quartered

½ cucumber, peeled, deseeded and chopped

150 g / 5 ½ oz / ⅔ cup feta, broken into chunks

2 handfuls of basil leaves

3 tbsp extra virgin olive oil

black pepper

METHOD

- Preheat the oven to 220°C (200°C fan) / 425F / gas 7.

- Brush the lamb with tahini paste, then roll in the ras el hanout to coat. Transfer the racks to a roasting tin and roast in the oven for 15 minutes.

- Cover the lamb with a double layer of foil and leave to rest for 5 minutes.

- Toss the chickpeas, tomatoes, cucumber, feta and basil together and arrange on a large serving platter. Cut the lamb into 2-bone cutlets and position on top of the salad, then dress with olive oil and black pepper.

TOP TIP
Scatter over the seeds of a pomegranate.

Mussel Chowder

SERVES 4

PREPARATION TIME 15 MINUTES

COOKING TIME 15 MINUTES

INGREDIENTS

2 tbsp butter

2 shallots, finely chopped

2 cloves of garlic, crushed

175 ml / 6 fl. oz / ⅔ cup dry white wine

1.2 litres / 2 pints / 4 ¾ cups live mussels, scrubbed

250 ml / 9 fl. oz / 1 cup fish stock

250 ml / 9 fl. oz / 1 cup double (heavy) cream

1 tbsp flat leaf parsley, chopped

salt and black pepper

METHOD

- Heat the butter in a large saucepan and fry the shallots and garlic for 5 minutes without colouring. Pour in the white wine and bring to the boil, then add the mussels and put on the lid.

- Steam the mussels in the pan for 6 minutes or until they have all opened. Strain the mussels through a large sieve, collecting all the liquid in a clean saucepan. Stir the fish stock and cream into the saucepan and heat gently.

- Pick the mussel meat from the shells, dropping them into the saucepan as you go. Discard the shells. Bring the chowder to a gentle simmer, then taste for seasoning and adjust with salt and pepper.

- Ladle the chowder into 4 warm bowls and garnish with parsley.

TOP TIP

Serve the chowder with lots of crusty bread for mopping up the juices.

Oriental Chicken with Asparagus

SERVES 2
PREPARATION TIME 1 HOUR 10 MINUTES
COOKING TIME 10 MINUTES

INGREDIENTS

2 tbsp sesame oil
1 tsp Szechuan peppercorns, crushed
1 clove of garlic, crushed
1 tsp fresh root ginger, finely grated
2 skinless chicken breasts
10 asparagus spears, trimmed
2 tbsp vegetable oil
4 tbsp oyster sauce
3 spring onions (scallions), sliced diagonally
rice noodles to serve

METHOD

- Mix the sesame oil with the peppercorns, garlic and ginger and rub it into the chicken and asparagus. Leave to marinate for 1 hour.

- Heat the vegetable oil in a large frying pan and gently fry the chicken and asparagus for 8 minutes or until the chicken is cooked through, turning occasionally.

- Stir 4 tbsp of water into the oyster sauce then add it to the pan. Bubble for 1 minute, turning the chicken and asparagus to coat.

- Sprinkle the spring onions over the chicken and serve with rice noodles.

TOP TIP
Try using purple sprouting broccoli when asparagus isn't in season.

Rosemary-roasted Beef Fillet

SERVES 6
PREPARATION TIME 1 HOUR 20 MINUTES
COOKING TIME 35 MINUTES

INGREDIENTS

6 tbsp olive oil
1 clove of garlic, finely chopped
3 tbsp rosemary, roughly chopped
1 kg / 2 lb 3 oz / 4 cups fillet of beef
2 red peppers, deseeded and cut into wedges
2 yellow pepper, deseeded and cut into wedges
2 green peppers, deseeded and cut into wedges

METHOD

- Preheat the oven to 230°C (210°C fan) / 450F / gas 8.

- Mix of half the oil with the garlic and rosemary and season well with salt and pepper. Rub the mixture into the beef and leave to marinate for 1 hour.

- Transfer the beef to a roasting tin and roast for 35 minutes.

- Meanwhile, heat a griddle pan until smoking hot. Rub the rest of the oil into the peppers and season with salt and pepper. Griddle the peppers for 10 minutes or until nicely charred in places, turning occasionally.

- Move the beef to a warm plate, wrap with a double layer of foil and leave to rest for 10 minutes before carving into thick slices and serving with the peppers.

TOP TIP
Try griddling aubergines and courgettes with the peppers.

Chicken and Vegetable Stew

SERVES 4
PREPARATION TIME 5 MINUTES
COOKING TIME 20 MINUTES

INGREDIENTS

2 tbsp olive oil
450 g / 1 lb / 2 cups chicken breast, cubed
1 leek, sliced
1 celery stick, diced
2 cloves of garlic, crushed
400 g / 14 oz / 2 cups canned tomatoes,
    chopped
600 ml / 1 pint / 2 ½ cups chicken stock
1 lemon, juiced and zest finely grated
2 tbsp flat leaf parsley, chopped
salt and black pepper

METHOD

- Heat the oil in a wide saucepan and sear the chicken pieces all over. Remove to a plate with a slotted spoon.

- Add the leek, celery and garlic to the pan and cook without colouring for 5 minutes. Pour in the tomatoes and stock and bring to the boil, then return the chicken to the pan and simmer gently for 10 minutes.

- Stir the lemon juice and zest into the stew and add salt and pepper to taste. Sprinkle over the parsley and serve immediately.

TOP TIP
This recipe also works well with firm-fleshed fish in place of the chicken.

Chunky Vegetable Soup

SERVES 4
PREPARATION TIME 15 MINUTES
COOKING TIME 30 MINUTES

INGREDIENTS

2 tbsp olive oil
2 tbsp butter
1 leek, chopped
2 cloves of garlic, crushed
2 carrots, chopped
1 celery stick, chopped
1 large potato, cubed
2 courgettes (zucchinis), chopped
1 litre / 1 pint 15 fl. oz / 4 cups vegetable stock
salt and black pepper

METHOD

- Heat the oil and butter in a saucepan and fry the leek for 8 minutes or until softened.

- Add the garlic and the rest of the vegetables to the pan and cook for 2 more minutes, then stir in the vegetable stock and bring to the boil. Simmer for 20 minutes.

- Ladle half of the soup into a liquidiser and blend until smooth, then stir it back into the saucepan.

- Season to taste with salt and pepper, then ladle into bowls and serve.

TOP TIP
Stir a spoonful of pesto into each bowl for depth of flavour.

Squash Stuffed with Bean Stew

SERVES 4

PREPARATION TIME 20 MINUTES

COOKING TIME 45 MINUTES

INGREDIENTS

2 tbsp olive oil

1 onion, finely chopped

2 cloves of garlic, crushed

400 g / 14 oz / 2 cups canned tomatoes,
    chopped

400 g / 14 oz / 2 cups canned haricot beans,
    drained

4 small squash

a handful of basil leaves

salt and black pepper

METHOD

- Preheat the oven to 180°C (160°C fan) / 350F / gas 4.

- Heat the oil in a saucepan and fry the onion for 5 minutes or until softened. Add the garlic and cook for 2 more minutes then stir in the tomatoes and beans. Season to taste with salt and pepper.

- Cut the tops off the squash then scoop out and discard the seeds. Stir the basil into the tomato mixture, then spoon it into the squash and replace the lids.

- Transfer the squash to a roasting tin then bake for 45 minutes or until a skewer will pass through the side of the squash easily.

TOP TIP

Stir in 150 ml of double (heavy) cream and top with mozzarella before baking.

Salmon with Bean Stew

SERVES 4

PREPARATION TIME 5 MINUTES

COOKING TIME 25 MINUTES

INGREDIENTS

2 tbsp olive oil

1 fennel bulb, quartered and sliced

1 green pepper, deseeded, quartered and sliced

3 cloves of garlic, finely chopped

400 g / 14 oz / 2 cups canned tomatoes, chopped

400 g / 14 oz / 2 cups canned cannellini beans, drained

4 portions salmon fillet

2 tsp fennel seeds

lemon wedges and chive shoots to serve

salt and black pepper

METHOD

- Preheat the oven to 180°C (160°C fan) / 350F / gas 4.

- Heat the oil in a saucepan and fry the fennel and pepper for 5 minutes or until softened. Add the garlic and cook for 2 more minutes then stir in the tomatoes and beans. Season to taste with salt and pepper then simmer gently while you cook the salmon.

- Sprinkle the salmon with fennel seeds then bake in a baking dish for 15 minutes or until the centre has only just turned opaque. Sprinkle the salmon with chive shoots and serve with the beans and lemon wedges on the side.

TOP TIP

This recipe also works well with chickpeas instead of the beans.

Beef and Vegetable Ragu

SERVES 5

PREPARATION TIME 5 MINUTES

COOKING TIME 1 HOUR 15 MINUTES

INGREDIENTS

2 tbsp olive oil

½ onion, chopped

½ carrot, chopped

½ celery stick, chopped

2 cloves of garlic, crushed

250 g / 9 oz / 1 ¼ cups minced beef

3 large portabello mushrooms, chopped

400 g / 14 oz / 1 ¾ cups canned tomatoes, chopped

150 ml / 5 ½ fl. oz / ⅔ cup beef stock

400 g / 14 oz / 2 cups dried spaghetti

3 tbsp black olives, pitted and chopped

a small bunch of basil, torn

METHOD

- Heat the oil in a large saucepan and fry the onion, carrot and celery for 5 minutes, stirring occasionally. Add the garlic and cook for 2 minutes, then add the mince and mushrooms.

- Fry until the mince starts to brown then add the chopped tomatoes and stock and bring to a gentle simmer. Cook for 1 hour, stirring occasionally, until the mince is tender and the sauce has thickened a little.

- Boil the pasta in salted water according to the packet instructions or until al dente. Drain well.

- Stir the olives and basil into the sauce and serve with the spaghetti.

TOP TIP

Substitute the beef with vegetarian mince.

Chicken Curry

SERVES 4

PREPARATION TIME 5 MINUTES

COOKING TIME 15 MINUTES

INGREDIENTS

2 tbsp sunflower oil

1 onion, thinly sliced

2 cloves of garlic, finely chopped

2.5 cm (1 in) piece fresh root ginger,
    finely chopped

1 red pepper, deseeded and thinly sliced

2 tbsp curry powder

2 kaffir lime leaves

400 ml / 14 fl. oz / 1 ⅔ cups chicken stock

200 ml / 7 fl. oz / ¾ cup coconut milk

225 g / 8 oz / 1 cup chicken breast, cubed

1 lime, juiced

coriander (cilantro leaves) to garnish

steamed rice and chilli (chili) chutney
    to serve

poppadoms

salt

METHOD

- Heat the oil in a saucepan and fry the onion, garlic, ginger and pepper for 5 minutes. Sprinkle in the curry powder and add the lime leaves and fry for 1 more minute, then pour in the stock and coconut milk.

- Bring the liquid to the boil, then stir in the chicken and poach gently for 5 minutes. Try the sauce and add salt and lime juice to taste.

- Garnish the curry with coriander leaves and serve with steamed rice, poppadoms and chilli chutney.

TOP TIP
Substitute the chicken with roasted aubergine and use vegetable stock.

Steak with Garlic Butter and Potato Wedges

SERVES 2
PREPARATION TIME 10 MINUTES
COOKING TIME 15 MINUTES

INGREDIENTS

sunflower oil for deep-frying

4 medium potatoes, cut into wedges

2 T-bone steaks

2 tbsp butter, softened

1 clove of garlic, crushed

1 tbsp flat leaf parsley, finely chopped

salad leaves to serve

salt and black pepper

METHOD

- Preheat the grill to its highest setting and heat the oil in a deep fat fryer, according to the manufacturer's instructions, to a temperature of 130°C.

- Lower the potato wedges in the fryer basket and cook for 10 minutes so that they cook all the way through but don't brown.

- Pull up the fryer basket and increase the fryer temperature to 190°C. When the oil has come up to temperature, lower the fryer basket and cook the wedges for 5 minutes or until crisp and golden brown.

- While the wedges are cooking, season the steaks with salt and pepper and grill for 4 minutes on each side or until cooked to your liking. Leave to rest somewhere warm while you finish the wedges.

- Mix the butter with the garlic and parsley, then shape into 2 butter pats.

- Top each steak with a garlic butter and serve with the wedges and salad leaves.

TOP TIP

Try mashing a little blue cheese into the butter for a tasty treat.

Chicken, Tomato and Avocado Baguette

SERVES 2

PREPARATION TIME 5 MINUTES

COOKING TIME 4 MINUTES

INGREDIENTS

1 skinless chicken breast

1 tbsp olive oil

1 baguette, halved

2 tbsp mayonnaise

½ tomato, sliced

½ avocado, stoned, skinned and sliced

a handful of baby spinach leaves

salt and black pepper

METHOD

- Heat a cast iron griddle pan until smoking hot.

- Slice the chicken breast in half horizontally to make 2 thin escalopes. Brush the chicken with oil and season with salt and pepper, then griddle for 2 minutes on each side or until cooked through.

- Split open the baguette halves and spread the inside with mayonnaise. Stuff with the chicken, tomato, avocado and salad leaves and serve straight away.

TOP TIP
Add a few rashers of crispy bacon to each sandwich for a great texture contrast.

Vegetarian Penne Bolognese

SERVES 4

PREPARATION TIME 5 MINUTES

COOKING TIME 25 MINUTES

INGREDIENTS

2 tbsp olive oil

½ onion, finely chopped

½ carrot, finely chopped

½ celery stick, finely chopped

2 cloves of garlic, crushed

2 tsp dried oregano

250 g / 9 oz / 1 ¼ cups vegetarian mince

400 g / 14 oz / 1 ¾ cups canned tomatoes, chopped

400 g / 14 oz / 4 cups dried penne

Parmesan shavings and basil leaves to garnish

METHOD

- Heat the oil in a large saucepan and fry the onion, carrot and celery for 5 minutes, stirring occasionally. Add the garlic and oregano and cook for 2 minutes, then add the mince.

- Fry until the mince starts to brown then add the chopped tomatoes and bring to a gentle simmer. Cook for 15 minutes.

- Meanwhile, boil the pasta in salted water according to the packet instructions or until al dente. Drain well.

- Serve the sauce on top of the pasta and garnish with Parmesan shavings and basil leaves.

TOP TIP

Top with mozzarella, then bake for 20 minutes.

Vegetable and Rosemary Skewers

SERVES 4

PREPARATION TIME 15 MINUTES

COOKING TIME 20 MINUTES

INGREDIENTS

12 waxy new potatoes, halved

8 long woody rosemary sprigs

2 red onions, cut into chunks

2 red peppers, deseeded and cut into chunks

3 tbsp olive oil

salt and black pepper

METHOD

- Cook the potatoes in salted boiling water for 12 minutes or until just tender. Drain well.

- Preheat the grill to its highest setting.

- Remove most of the leaves from the rosemary sprigs, then thread the potatoes, onion and peppers onto the stems.

- Brush the vegetables with oil and season with salt and pepper, then grill for 4 minutes on each side or until lightly charred in places. Serve immediately.

TOP TIP

Try adding chunks of halloumi cheese to the skewers.

Watercress, Pear and Goats' Cheese Soup

SERVES 4

PREPARATION TIME 10 MINUTES

COOKING TIME 10 MINUTES

INGREDIENTS

2 tbsp olive oil

2 tbsp butter

1 small onion, chopped

2 cloves of garlic, crushed

1 litre / 1 pint 15 fl. oz / 4 cups vegetable stock

200 g / 7 oz / 6 cups watercress, washed

4 tbsp soft goats' cheese

1 ripe pear, cored, quartered and thinly sliced

2 tbsp Parmesan, grated

salt and black pepper

METHOD

- Heat the oil and butter in a saucepan and fry the onion and garlic for 5 minutes or until softened, but not coloured.

- Pour in the vegetable stock and bring to the boil, then stir in the watercress, reserving a few leaves to garnish. As soon as the stock comes back to the boil, ladle the soup into a liquidiser and blend until smooth. Season to taste with salt and pepper.

- Ladle the soup into 4 warm bowls and top with the watercress leaves, goats' cheese, pear and Parmesan.

TOP TIP

This recipe also works well with spinach.

Prawn and Chorizo Paella

SERVES 4

PREPARATION TIME 15 MINUTES

COOKING TIME 25 MINUTES

INGREDIENTS

1 litre / 1 pint 15 fl. oz / 4 cups chicken stock
4 tbsp olive oil
1 onion, finely chopped
2 cloves of garlic, crushed
1 yellow pepper, deseeded and sliced
100 g / 3 ½ oz / ⅔ cup chorizo, diced
100 g / 3 ½ oz / ⅔ cup frozen peas, defrosted
200 g / 7 oz / 1 cup paella rice
200 g / 7 oz / 1 cup raw prawns, peeled
lemon wedges to garnish
salt and black pepper

METHOD

- Heat the stock in a saucepan.

- Heat the olive oil in a paella pan and gently fry the onion, garlic, pepper and chorizo for 5 minutes without colouring.

- Stir in the peas and rice and season with salt and pepper. Stir well to coat with the oil, then pour in the hot stock and stir once more.

- Simmer without stirring for 10 minutes or until there's only just enough stock left to cover the rice. Distribute the prawns evenly across the surface and press them down into the liquid. Simmer without stirring for 5 more minutes.

- Cover the pan with foil or a lid, turn off the heat and leave to stand for 5 minutes. Serve with lemon wedges to garnish.

TOP TIP
Add a handful of live mussels and clams 5 minutes before the end of cooking.

Tomato Soup

SERVES 4
PREPARATION TIME 10 MINUTES
COOKING TIME 30 MINUTES

INGREDIENTS

400 g / 14 oz / 2 cups ripe tomatoes
2 tbsp olive oil
1 onion, finely chopped
2 cloves of garlic, crushed
1 tbsp tomato purée
1 litre / 1 pint 15 fl. oz / 4 cups vegetable stock
4 tbsp double (heavy) cream
2 tbsp flat leaf parsley, chopped
salt and black pepper

METHOD

- Score a cross in the top of the tomatoes and blanch them in boiling water for 30 seconds. Plunge them into cold water then peel off the skins. Cut the tomatoes in half and remove the seeds, then cut the flesh into small cubes.

- Heat the oil in a saucepan and fry the onion for 5 minutes or until softened. Add the garlic and cook for 2 more minutes then stir in the tomatoes and tomato purée. Pour in the vegetable stock and bring to the boil.

- Simmer for 20 minutes then blend until smooth with a stick blender. Taste the soup and adjust the seasoning with salt and pepper.

- Ladle the soup into 4 warm bowls and stir a little cream into the top of each one. Garnish with parsley and grind over a little black pepper.

TOP TIP
Try garnishing the soup with basil instead of parsley.

Salmon and Vegetable Stew

SERVES 4

PREPARATION TIME 5 MINUTES

COOKING TIME 30 MINUTES

INGREDIENTS

2 tbsp olive oil

1 onion, finely chopped

2 cloves of garlic, crushed

2 large potatoes, peeled and cubed

1 green romano pepper, deseeded and sliced

1 bay leaf

600 ml / 1 pint / 2 ½ cups fish stock

400 g / 14 oz / 2 cups canned tomatoes, chopped

4 thick salmon steaks

salt and black pepper

METHOD

- Heat the oil in a wide saucepan and fry the onion for 5 minutes or until softened. Add the garlic and cook for 2 more minutes then stir in the potatoes, pepper and bay leaf.

- Pour in the stock and tomatoes and bring to the boil. Season to taste with salt and pepper.

- Simmer for 15 minutes, then add the salmon steaks and push them down into the liquid. Cover the pan and simmer very gently for 5 minutes or until the salmon is just cooked in the centre and the potatoes are tender. Serve immediately.

TOP TIP
This recipe works really well with small whole rainbow trout instead of the salmon.

Roasted Quail and Fig Salad

SERVES 4

PREPARATION TIME 10 MINUTES

COOKING TIME 20 MINUTES

INGREDIENTS

4 quail, quartered

6 figs, quartered

2 thick slices sourdough bread, torn into chunks

3 tbsp olive oil

75 g / 2 ½ oz / ½ cup feta, crumbled

3 tbsp pomegranate seeds

3 tbsp walnut pieces

a small handful of flat leaf parsley leaves

a handful of baby leaf spinach

½ radicchio lettuce, chopped

salt and black pepper

METHOD

- Preheat the oven to 200°C (180°C fan) / 400F / gas 6.

- Rub the quail, figs and bread with oil and spread them out in a roasting tin. Season with salt and pepper then roast for 20 minutes or until the quail is cooked through.

- Stir the rest of the ingredients into the roasting tin, then divide between 4 warm bowls and serve immediately.

TOP TIP

If you aren't able to source quail, use poussin instead.

Stuffed Roast Chicken

SERVES 4

PREPARATION TIME 45 MINUTES

COOKING TIME 1 HOUR 20 MINUTES

INGREDIENTS

2 tbsp butter

1 onion, finely chopped

2 cloves of garlic, crushed

75 g / 2 ½ oz / 1 cup fresh breadcrumbs

2 tbsp sage leaves, finely chopped

1.5 kg / 3 lb 5 oz / 6 cups oven-ready chicken

75 ml / 2 ½ fl. oz / ⅓ cup dry white wine

salt

METHOD

- Preheat the oven to 200°C (180°C fan) / 400F / gas 6.

- Heat the butter in a frying pan and fry the onion and garlic with a big pinch of salt for 5 minutes or until softened.

- Take the pan off the heat and stir in the breadcrumbs and sage. Leave to cool.

- Insert your fingers between the skin and flesh of the chicken breast to create a pocket, and do the same with the legs.

- Pack the stuffing into the pockets you've created and smooth the skin flat again. Transfer the chicken to a roasting tin and pour the wine around it.

- Roast the chicken for 30 minutes, then turn the heat down to 170°C (150°C fan) / 340F / gas 3 and roast for a further 50 minutes. To test if the chicken is cooked, insert a skewer into the thickest part of the thigh. If the juices run clear, the chicken is cooked.

- Cover the chicken with a double layer of foil and a thick tea towel and leave to rest for 20 minutes before carving and serving.

TOP TIP

Add 4 chopped rashers of bacon and a handful of chopped chestnuts to the stuffing.

Italian Stuffed Sea Bass

SERVES 6

PREPARATION TIME 25 MINUTES

COOKING TIME 35 MINUTES

INGREDIENTS

8 slices prosciutto

1 large sea bass, filleted, skinned and pin-boned

2 mild red chillies (chilies), sliced

2 cloves of garlic, finely chopped

3 tbsp flat leaf parsley, chopped

3 tbsp olive oil

1 tsp coriander (cilantro) seeds

2 carrots, chopped

1 celery stick, chopped

150 g / 5 ½ oz / 2 cups button mushrooms, quartered

175 ml / 6 fl. oz / ⅔ cup dry white wine

salt and black pepper

METHOD

- Preheat the oven to 200°C (180°C fan) / 400F / gas 6.

- Lay out the prosciutto in a single, overlapping layer on a chopping board. Lay one of the sea bass fillets on top and sprinkle over the chilli, garlic and parsley. Season with salt and pepper. Sandwich with the other sea bass fillet and wrap the prosciutto around it. Tie securely with string in several places along the length.

- Heat the oil in a frying pan and add the coriander seeds, then fry the carrots, celery and mushrooms for 5 minutes. Pour in the wine and simmer for 2 minutes, then scrape the mixture into a baking dish.

- Sit the sea bass on top of the vegetables then transfer the dish to the oven and bake for 25 minutes or until the fish is just cooked in the centre.

- Cut the fish into thick slices and serve with the vegetables.

TOP TIP

Try with any firm-fleshed fish — bream or snapper work really well.

Breads

Parmesan Baguettes

MAKES 2

PREPARATION TIME 2 HOURS 30 MINUTES

COOKING TIME 25 MINUTES

INGREDIENTS

350 g / 12 ½ oz / 1 ½ cups strong white bread
flour, plus extra for dusting

50 g / 1 ¾ oz / ⅓ cup stoneground wholemeal
flour

½ tsp easy-blend dried yeast

50 g / 1 ¾ oz / ½ cup Parmesan, finely grated

1 tsp fine sea salt

1 tbsp olive oil

METHOD

- Mix together the flours, yeast, Parmesan and salt. Stir the oil into 280 ml / 10 fl. oz / 1 ⅛ cups of warm water then stir it into the dry ingredients.

- Knead the mixture on a lightly oiled surface for 10 minutes or until smooth and elastic. Leave the dough to rest, covered with oiled cling film, for 1–2 hours or until doubled in size.

- Roll the dough into 2 baguettes and taper the ends to a point.

- Transfer the baguettes to a greased baking tray then cover with oiled cling film and leave to prove for 1 hour or until doubled in size.

- Preheat the oven to 220°C (200°C fan) / 425F / gas 7.

- Dust the baguettes with a little flour and make a few diagonal slashes along the top with a sharp knife. Place the tray on the top shelf of the oven.

- Bake for 25 minutes or until the baguettes sounds hollow when you tap them underneath. Transfer to a wire rack and leave to cool completely before serving.

TOP TIP

Serve these baguettes as an accompaniment to Italian-style soups and stews.

Poppy Seed Rolls

MAKES 16

PREPARATION TIME 2 HOURS 30 MINUTES

COOKING TIME 15 MINUTES

INGREDIENTS

400 g / 14 oz / 2 ⅔ cups strong white bread
  flour, plus extra for dusting

½ tsp easy-blend dried yeast

1 tbsp caster (superfine) sugar

1 tsp fine sea salt

1 tbsp olive oil

1 egg, beaten

3 tbsp poppy seeds

METHOD

- Mix together the flour, yeast, sugar and salt. Stir the oil into 280 ml / 10 fl. oz / 1 ⅛ cups of warm water then stir it into the dry ingredients.

- Knead the mixture on a lightly oiled surface for 10 minutes or until smooth and elastic. Leave the dough to rest in a lightly oiled bowl, covered with oiled cling film, for 1–2 hours or until doubled in size.

- Knead the dough for 2 more minutes then split it into 16 even pieces and shape into rolls. Press your finger into the centre of each roll to produce a deep dimple. Transfer the rolls to a greased baking tray and cover with oiled cling film. Leave to prove for 1 hour or until doubled in size.

- Meanwhile, preheat the oven to 220°C (200°C fan) / 425F / gas 7.

- Brush the rolls with beaten egg and sprinkle with poppy seeds. Place the tray on the top shelf of the oven. Bake for 15 minutes or until the rolls sound hollow when you tap them underneath. Transfer to a wire rack and leave to cool completely.

TOP TIP
These rolls are delicious filled with tuna and sweetcorn mayonnaise.

Thyme Fougasse

MAKES 2

PREPARATION TIME 2 HOURS 30 MINUTES

COOKING TIME 25 MINUTES

INGREDIENTS

400 g / 14 oz / 2 ⅔ cups strong white bread
   flour, plus extra for dusting

½ tsp easy-blend dried yeast

2 tsp dried thyme

1 tsp fine sea salt

3 tbsp olive oil, plus extra for brushing

METHOD

- Mix together the flours, yeast, thyme and salt. Stir the oil into 280 ml / 10 fl. oz / 1 ⅛ cups of warm water then stir it into the dry ingredients.

- Knead the mixture on a lightly oiled surface for 10 minutes or until smooth and elastic. Leave the dough to rest, covered with oiled cling film, for 1–2 hours or until doubled in size.

- Divide the dough into 2 pieces and shape each piece into a leaf shape, making deep slashes where the veins would be. Transfer the fougasse to a greased baking tray then cover with oiled cling film and leave to prove for 1 hour or until doubled in size.

- Preheat the oven to 220°C (200°C fan) / 425F / gas 7.

- Bake on the top shelf of the oven for 25 minutes or until the loaves sounds hollow when you tap them underneath. Transfer to a wire rack and brush with olive oil, then leave to cool completely before serving.

TOP TIP

Add a handful of finely diced chorizo for a spicy flavour.

Seeded Rolls

MAKES 8 ROLLS

PREPARATION TIME 2 HOURS 30 MINUTES

COOKING TIME 12 MINUTES

INGREDIENTS

400 g / 14 oz / 2 ⅔ cups strong white bread
    flour, plus extra for dusting

2 tbsp sunflower seeds

2 tbsp linseeds seeds

1 tbsp pumpkin seeds

½ tsp easy-blend dried yeast

1 tbsp caster (superfine) sugar

1 tsp fine sea salt

1 tbsp olive oil

METHOD

- Mix together the flour, seeds, yeast, sugar and salt. Stir the oil into 280 ml / 10 fl. oz / 1 ⅛ cups of warm water then stir the liquid into the dry ingredients.

- Knead the mixture on a lightly oiled surface for 10 minutes or until smooth and elastic. Leave the dough to rest, covered with oiled cling film, for 1–2 hours or until doubled in size.

- Divide the dough into 8 evenly-sized pieces and shape into rolls on a greased baking tray. Cover the rolls with oiled cling film and leave to prove for 1 hour or until doubled in size.

- Preheat the oven to 220°C (200°C fan) / 430F / gas 7.

- Place the tray on the top shelf of the oven. Bake for 12 minutes or until the rolls sound hollow when you tap them underneath.

TOP TIP
Try filling the rolls
with pulled pork and
homemade coleslaw.

Baguettes

MAKES 2
PREPARATION TIME 2 HOURS 30 MINUTES
COOKING TIME 25 MINUTES

INGREDIENTS

350 g / 12 ½ oz / 1 ½ cups strong white bread flour, plus extra for dusting

50 g / 1 ¾ oz / ¼ cup stoneground wholemeal flour

½ tsp easy-blend dried yeast

1 tbsp caster (superfine) sugar

1 tsp fine sea salt

1 tbsp olive oil

METHOD

- Mix together the flours, yeast, sugar and salt. Stir the oil into 280 ml / 10 fl. oz / 1 ⅛ cups of warm water then stir it into the dry ingredients.

- Knead the mixture on a lightly oiled surface for 10 minutes or until smooth and elastic. Leave the dough to rest, covered with oiled cling film, for 1–2 hours or until doubled in size.

- Roll the dough into a long baguette, then make a diagonal cut half way down to form 2 shorter baguettes.

- Transfer the baguettes to a greased baking tray then cover with oiled cling film and leave to prove for 1 hour or until doubled in size.

- Preheat the oven to 220°C (200°C fan) / 425F / gas 7.

- Dust the baguettes with a little flour and make a few diagonal slashes along the top with a sharp knife.

- Bake on the top shelf of the oven for 25 minutes or until the baguettes sound hollow when you tap them underneath. Transfer to a wire rack and leave to cool completely before serving.

TOP TIP
Serve for breakfast with unsalted butter and strawberry jam (jelly).

Kamut Batons

MAKES 4

PREPARATION TIME 2–3 HOURS

COOKING TIME 20 MINUTES

INGREDIENTS

200 g / 7 oz / 1 ⅓ cups kamut flour

200 g / 7 oz / 1 ⅓ cups strong white bread
flour, plus extra for dusting

½ tsp easy-blend dried yeast

2 tbsp caster (superfine) sugar

1 tsp fine sea salt

1 tbsp olive oil

METHOD

- Mix together the flours, yeast, sugar and salt. Stir the oil into 280 ml / 10 fl. oz / 1 ⅛ cups of warm water then stir it into the dry ingredients.

- Knead the mixture on a lightly oiled surface with your hands for 10 minutes or until smooth and elastic. Leave the dough to rest in a lightly oiled bowl, covered with oiled cling film, for 1–2 hours or until doubled in size.

- Knead it for 2 more minutes and then divide it into 4 pieces and shape into batons. Transfer the batons to a greased baking tray and cover with oiled cling film. Leave to prove for 1 hour or until doubled in size.

- Meanwhile, preheat the oven to 220°C (200°C fan) / 425F / gas 7.

- Make 3 diagonal slashes across the top of each baton with a sharp knife. Transfer the tray to the top shelf of the oven. Bake for 20 minutes or until the loaves sound hollow when you tap them underneath. Transfer to a wire rack and leave to cool completely.

TOP TIP

Try filling the batons with salami and antipasti.

Tomato and Olive Bread

MAKES 2 LOAVES

PREPARATION TIME 2–3 HOURS

COOKING TIME 35 MINUTES

INGREDIENTS

400 g / 14 oz / 2 ⅔ cups strong white bread
    flour, plus extra for dusting

½ tsp easy-blend dried yeast

1 tbsp caster (superfine) sugar

1 tsp fine sea salt

100 g / 3 ½ oz / ⅔ cup mixed olives, pitted
    and sliced

100 g / 3 ½ oz / ½ cup sun-dried tomatoes in
    oil, drained and finely chopped

1 tbsp oil from the sun-dried tomatoes

METHOD

- In a large bowl, mix together the
  flour, yeast, sugar and salt. Stir the
  olives, tomatoes and their oil into
  280 ml / 10 fl. oz / 1 ⅛ cups of warm
  water. Stir the liquid into the dry
  ingredients then knead the mixture
  on a lightly oiled surface with your
  hands for 10 minutes or until the
  dough is smooth and elastic.

- Leave the dough to rest in a lightly
  oiled bowl, covered with oiled cling
  film, for 1–2 hours or until doubled
  in size. Knead it briefly again, then
  divide in half and roll out into a fat
  sausage. Fold each sausage round
  into a 'S' shape then transfer to a
  greased baking tray and cover with
  oiled cling film. Leave to prove for
  1 hour or until doubled in size.

- Meanwhile, preheat the oven to
  220°C (200°C fan) / 425F / gas 7.

- Transfer the tray to the top shelf of
  the oven. Bake for 35 minutes or
  until the loaves sound hollow when
  you tap them underneath. Transfer
  to a wire rack and leave to
  cool completely.

TOP TIP
This bread is delicious
served with a
Niçoise salad.

Ciabatta

MAKES 2

PREPARATION TIME 2 HOURS 30 MINUTES

COOKING TIME 20 MINUTES

INGREDIENTS

100 g / 3 ½ oz / ⅔ cup strong white bread
    flour

200 g / 7 oz / 1 ⅓ cups '00' pasta flour, plus
    extra for dusting

½ tsp easy-blend dried yeast

1 tsp fine sea salt

1 tbsp olive oil

METHOD

- Mix together the flours, yeast, salt and
  rosemary. Stir the oil into 280 ml / 10 fl.
  oz / 1 ⅛ cups of warm water then stir the
  liquid into the dry ingredients.

- The mixture will be stickier than normal
  bread dough, so knead it on a wet work
  surface with the help of 2 plastic scrapers
  for 10 minutes or until the dough is
  smooth and elastic. Divide the dough
  into two pieces and leave to rest on the
  worktop, covered with two upturned
  mixing bowls, for 1–2 hours or until
  doubled in size.

- Use the plastic scrapers to gently fold
  the top of the first piece of dough into
  the middle then repeat with the bottom.
  Fold in the sides in the same way. Flour
  the work surface next to the first ciabatta
  with flour and use the scrapers to gently
  roll the loaf onto it.

- Dust the top with more flour then scoop
  the loaf up with the scrapers and transfer
  it to a greased baking tray. Repeat with
  the remaining dough. Cover the loaves
  with oiled cling film and leave to prove
  for 1 hour or until doubled in size.

- Meanwhile, preheat the oven to 220°C
  (200°C fan) / 425F / gas 7.

- Bake on the top shelf of the oven for
  20 minutes then transfer the loaves to a
  wire rack and leave to cool completely.

TOP TIP

Drizzle with olive oil and
top with sliced tomatoes
and salt and pepper.

Flatbreads

MAKES 12

PREPARATION TIME 1–2 HOURS

COOKING TIME 25 MINUTES

INGREDIENTS

400 g / 14 oz / 2 ⅔ cups strong white bread
    flour, plus extra for dusting

½ tsp easy-blend dried yeast

1 tsp caster (superfine) sugar

1 tsp fine sea salt

4 tbsp natural yoghurt

2 tbsp olive oil

METHOD

- Mix together the flour, yeast, sugar and salt. Stir the yoghurt and oil into 200 ml / 7 fl. oz / ¾ cup of warm water then stir it into the dry ingredients.

- Knead the mixture on a lightly oiled surface for 10 minutes or until smooth and elastic. Leave the dough to rest, covered with oiled cling film, for 1–2 hours or until doubled in size.

- Divide the dough into 12 pieces then roll each one out into a thin circle.

- Heat a large frying pan over the hob, then lay your first flatbread on top and cook for 1 minute or until the underside just starts to colour. Turn the bread over and cook the other side, then lay it between 2 clean tea towels.

- Repeat with the rest of the dough circles, then serve straight away.

TOP TIP
Use the flatbreads as a wrap for falafel, hummus and pickles.

Small Brioche Loaves

MAKES 3

PREPARATION TIME 8 HOURS 30 MINUTES

COOKING TIME 20 MINUTES

INGREDIENTS

250 g / 9 oz / 1 ¼ cups butter, cubed

400 g / 14 oz / 2 ⅔ cups strong white bread
flour

2 ½ tsp easy-blend dried yeast

4 tbsp caster (superfine) sugar

1 tsp fine sea salt

4 large eggs, plus 3 egg yolks

METHOD

- Rub the butter into the flour then stir in the yeast, sugar and salt. Beat the whole eggs and yolks together and stir into the dry ingredients.

- Beat the dough with a wooden spoon for 8 minutes, as it will be too soft to knead. Cover the bowl with cling film, then leave to prove slowly in the fridge for 6 hours or until doubled in size.

- Knead the dough for 5 minutes, then divide it between 3 small loaf tins. Cover with oiled cling film and leave to prove for 2 hours or until doubled in size.

- Meanwhile, preheat the oven to 220°C (200°C fan) / 425F / gas 7.

- Bake the brioche for 10 minutes, then reduce the heat to 190°C (170°C fan) / 375F / gas 5 and bake for a further 10 minutes or until the underneath of each loaf sounds hollow when tapped. Turn the loaves out onto a wire rack and leave to cool completely before serving.

TOP TIP

Serve these little loaves with jam (jelly) for dipping.

Crusty Lemon Rolls

MAKES 4

PREPARATION TIME 2 HOURS 30 MINUTES

COOKING TIME 20 MINUTES

INGREDIENTS

400 g / 14 oz / 2 ⅔ cups strong white bread
    flour, plus extra for dusting

½ tsp easy-blend dried yeast

1 tbsp caster (superfine) sugar

1 tsp fine sea salt

1 lemon, juiced and zest finely grated

1 tbsp olive oil

METHOD

- Mix together the flour, yeast, sugar, salt and lemon zest. Stir the oil and lemon juice into 250 ml / 9 fl. oz / 1 cup of warm water then stir it into the dry ingredients.

- Knead the mixture on a lightly oiled surface for 10 minutes or until smooth and elastic. Leave the dough to rest, covered with oiled cling film, for 1–2 hours or until doubled in size.

- Shape the dough into 4 long rolls and transfer to a greased baking tray, then cover with oiled cling film and leave to prove for 1 hour or until doubled in size.

- Preheat the oven to 220°C (200°C fan) / 425F / gas 7.

- Slash the top of each roll diagonally with a sharp knife. Bake on the top oven shelf for 20 minutes or until the rolls sound hollow when you tap them underneath. Transfer to a wire rack and leave to cool before serving.

TOP TIP
Try filling these rolls with smoked salmon and cream cheese.

Wholemeal Caraway Batons

MAKES 2

PREPARATION TIME 2 HOURS 30 MINUTES

COOKING TIME 30 MINUTES

INGREDIENTS

200 g / 7 oz / 1 ⅓ cups malted granary flour

200 g / 7 oz / 1 ⅓ cups wholemeal bread flour

½ tsp easy-blend dried yeast

1 tbsp caraway seeds

2 tbsp caster (superfine) sugar

1 tsp fine sea salt

1 tbsp olive oil

METHOD

- Mix together the flours, yeast, caraway, sugar and salt. Stir the oil into 280 ml / 10 fl. oz / 1 ⅛ cups of warm water then stir it into the dry ingredients.

- Knead the mixture on a lightly oiled surface with your hands for 10 minutes or until smooth and elastic. Leave the dough to rest in a lightly oiled bowl, covered with oiled cling film, for 1–2 hours or until doubled in size.

- Knead it for 2 more minutes then divide it into 2 pieces and shape into fat batons. Transfer the batons to a greased baking tray and cover with oiled cling film. Leave to prove for 1 hour or until doubled in size.

- Meanwhile, preheat the oven to 220°C (200°C fan) / 425F / gas 7.

- Make 2 diagonal slashes across the top of each baton with a sharp knife. Transfer the tray to the top shelf of the oven. Bake for 30 minutes or until the loaves sound hollow when you tap them underneath. Transfer to a wire rack and leave to cool completely.

TOP TIP

Serve the batons with vegetable soups.

Sweetcorn Rolls

MAKES 16

PREPARATION TIME 2–3 HOURS

COOKING TIME 15 MINUTES

INGREDIENTS

400 g / 14 oz / 2 ⅔ cups strong white bread
    flour, plus extra for dusting

½ tsp easy-blend dried yeast

1 tbsp caster (superfine) sugar

1 tsp fine sea salt

1 tbsp olive oil

100 g / 3 ½ oz / ½ cup canned sweetcorn,
    drained

METHOD

- Mix together the flour, yeast, sugar and salt. Stir the oil and sweetcorn into 280 ml / 10 fl. oz / 1 ⅛ cups of warm water then stir it into the dry ingredients.

- Knead the mixture on a lightly oiled surface for 10 minutes or until smooth and elastic. Leave the dough to rest in a lightly oiled bowl, covered with oiled cling film, for 1–2 hours or until doubled in size.

- Knead the dough for 2 more minutes then split it into 16 even pieces and shape into rolls. Transfer the rolls to a greased baking tray and cover with oiled cling film. Leave to prove for 1 hour or until doubled in size.

- Meanwhile, preheat the oven to 220°C (200°C fan) / 425F / gas 7.

- Transfer the tray to the top shelf of the oven. Bake for 15 minutes or until the rolls sound hollow when you tap them underneath. Transfer to a wire rack and leave to cool completely.

TOP TIP

These rolls taste great filled with spicy chicken and sliced avocado.

Seed-topped Square Rolls

MAKES 9 ROLLS

PREPARATION TIME 2 HOURS 30 MINUTES

COOKING TIME 12 MINUTES

INGREDIENTS

400 g / 14 oz / 2 ⅔ cups strong white bread flour, plus extra for dusting

½ tsp easy-blend dried yeast

1 tbsp caster (superfine) sugar

1 tsp fine sea salt

2 tbsp olive oil

2 tbsp milk

sesame seeds, poppy seeds and linseeds for sprinkling

METHOD

- Mix together the flour, yeast, sugar and salt. Stir the oil into 280 ml / 10 fl. oz / 1 ⅛ cups of warm water then stir the liquid into the dry ingredients.

- Knead the mixture on a lightly oiled surface for 10 minutes or until smooth and elastic. Leave the dough to rest, covered with oiled cling film, for 1–2 hours or until doubled in size.

- Roll out the dough into a square, then cut it into 9 rolls and transfer to a greased baking tray. Cover the rolls with oiled cling film and leave to prove for 1 hour or until doubled in size.

- Preheat the oven to 220°C (200°C fan) / 430F / gas 7.

- Brush the rolls with milk and sprinkle the tops with your choice of seeds. Transfer the tray to the top shelf of the oven. Bake for 12 minutes or until the rolls sound hollow when you tap them underneath.

TOP TIP

These little rolls taste great filled with sliced fresh figs and prosciutto.

Cheese and Bacon Bread

MAKES 1 LOAF

PREPARATION TIME 2–3 HOURS

COOKING TIME 35 MINUTES

INGREDIENTS

400 g / 14 oz / 2 ⅔ cups strong white bread
flour, plus extra for dusting

½ tsp easy-blend dried yeast

1 tbsp caster (superfine) sugar

1 tsp fine sea salt

100 g / 3 ½ oz / 1 cup streaky bacon, chopped

100 g / 3 ½ oz / 1 cup Cheddar, grated

a small bunch of chives, chopped

METHOD

- Mix together the flour, yeast, sugar and salt. Stir the bacon, cheese and chives into 280 ml / 10 fl. oz / 1 ⅛ cups of warm water and stir into the dry ingredients.

- Knead the mixture on a lightly oiled surface for 10 minutes or until the dough is smooth and elastic. Leave the dough to rest in a lightly oiled bowl, covered with oiled cling film, for 1–2 hours or until doubled in size.

- Knead the dough for 2 more minutes then roll it into a fat sausage. Turn it 90° and roll it tightly the other way then tuck the ends under and transfer the dough to a lined baking tray, keeping the seam underneath.

- Cover the dough loosely with oiled cling film and leave to prove for 45 minutes.

- Preheat the oven to 220°C (200°C fan) / 430F / gas 7.

- Transfer the tray to the top shelf of the oven. Bake for 35 minutes or until the underneath sounds hollow when tapped. Leave to cool completely on a wire rack before slicing.

TOP TIP
Try spreading the sliced bread with soft goats' cheese.

Sesame Granary Bread

MAKES 1

PREPARATION TIME 2–3 HOURS

COOKING TIME 30 MINUTES

INGREDIENTS

200 g / 7 oz / 1 ⅓ cups malted granary flour

200 g / 7 oz / 1 ⅓ cups strong white
  bread flour

½ tsp easy-blend dried yeast

2 tbsp caster (superfine) sugar

1 tsp fine sea salt

1 tbsp sesame oil

1 tbsp milk

2 tbsp sesame seeds

METHOD

- Mix together the flours, yeast, sugar and salt. Stir the oil into 280 ml / 10 fl. oz / 1 ⅛ cups of warm water then stir it into the dry ingredients.

- Knead the mixture on a lightly oiled surface with your hands for 10 minutes or until smooth and elastic. Leave the dough to rest in a lightly oiled bowl, covered with oiled cling film, for 1–2 hours or until doubled in size.

- Knead it for 2 more minutes then shape it into a long loaf and cover with oiled cling film. Leave to prove for 1 hour or until doubled in size.

- Meanwhile, preheat the oven to 220°C (200°C fan) / 425F / gas 7.

- Brush the loaf with milk and sprinkle with sesame seeds. Transfer the tray to the top shelf of the oven. Bake for 30 minutes or until the loaf sounds hollow when you tap it underneath. Transfer to a wire rack and leave to cool completely.

TOP TIP
This bread tastes really good made into a ham and mustard sandwich.

Wholemeal Granary Batons

MAKES 2

PREPARATION TIME 2–3 HOURS

COOKING TIME 30 MINUTES

INGREDIENTS

200 g / 7 oz / 1 ⅓ cups malted granary flour

200 g / 7 oz / 1 ⅓ cups wholemeal bread flour

½ tsp easy-blend dried yeast

2 tbsp caster (superfine) sugar

1 tsp fine sea salt

1 tbsp olive oil

METHOD

- Mix together the flours, yeast, sugar and salt. Stir the oil into 280 ml / 10 fl. oz / 1 ⅛ cups of warm water then stir it into the dry ingredients.

- Knead the mixture on a lightly oiled surface with your hands for 10 minutes or until smooth and elastic. Leave the dough to rest in a lightly oiled bowl, covered with oiled cling film, for 1–2 hours or until doubled in size.

- Knead it for 2 more minutes then divide it into 2 pieces and shape into fat batons. Transfer the batons to a greased baking tray and cover with oiled cling film. Leave to prove for 1 hour or until doubled in size.

- Meanwhile, preheat the oven to 220°C (200°C fan) / 425F / gas 7.

- Make 2 diagonal slashes across the top of each baton with a sharp knife. Transfer the tray to the top shelf of the oven. Bake for 30 minutes or until the loaves sound hollow when you tap them underneath. Transfer to a wire rack and leave to cool completely.

TOP TIP

Try filling these batons with crab mayonnaise and fresh mustard cress.

Walnut Brioche Loaf

MAKES 1

PREPARATION TIME 8–10 HOURS

COOKING TIME 30 MINUTES

INGREDIENTS

250 g / 9 oz / 1 ¼ cups butter, cubed

400 g / 14 oz / 2 ⅔ cups strong white
   bread flour

2 ½ tsp easy-blend dried yeast

4 tbsp caster (superfine) sugar

1 tsp fine sea salt

4 large eggs, plus 3 egg yolks

100 g / 3 ½ oz / ¾ cup walnuts, chopped

METHOD

- Rub the butter into the flour then stir in the yeast, sugar and salt. Beat the whole eggs and yolks together and stir into the dry ingredients with the walnuts.

- Beat the dough with a wooden spoon for 8 minutes, as it will be too soft to knead. Cover the bowl with cling film, then leave to prove slowly in the fridge for 6 hours or until doubled in size.

- Knead the dough for 5 minutes, then transfer it to a lined loaf tin. Cover with oiled cling film and leave to prove for 2 hours or until doubled in size.

- Meanwhile, preheat the oven to 220°C (200°C fan) / 425F / gas 7.

- Bake the brioche for 10 minutes, then reduce the heat to 190°C (170°C fan) / 375F / gas 5 and bake for a further 20 minutes or until the underneath sounds hollow when tapped. Turn the brioche out onto a wire rack and leave to cool completely before serving.

TOP TIP
Slice the brioche and serve with sliced bananas, cream cheese and honey.

Linseed Batons

MAKES 4

PREPARATION TIME 2–3 HOURS

COOKING TIME 20 MINUTES

INGREDIENTS

400 g / 14 oz / 2 ⅔ cups strong white bread
    flour, plus extra for dusting

½ tsp easy-blend dried yeast

2 tbsp caster (superfine) sugar

1 tsp fine sea salt

25 g / 1 oz / ¼ cup linseeds

1 tbsp linseed oil

METHOD

- Mix together the flour, yeast, sugar, salt and linseeds. Stir the oil into 280 ml / 10 fl. oz / 1 ⅛ cups of warm water then stir it into the dry ingredients.

- Knead the mixture on a lightly oiled surface with your hands for 10 minutes or until smooth and elastic. Leave the dough to rest in a lightly oiled bowl, covered with oiled cling film, for 1–2 hours or until doubled in size.

- Knead it for 2 more minutes then divide it into 4 pieces and shape into batons. Transfer the batons to a greased baking tray and cover with oiled cling film. Leave to prove for 1 hour or until doubled in size.

- Meanwhile, preheat the oven to 220°C (200°C fan) / 425F / gas 7.

- Make 2 diagonal slashes across the top of each baton with a sharp knife. Transfer the tray to the top shelf of the oven. Bake for 20 minutes or until the loaves sound hollow when you tap them underneath. Transfer to a wire rack and leave to cool completely.

TOP TIP
Try filling these batons with rare roast beef and horseradish sauce.

Crusty Rolls

MAKES 6

PREPARATION TIME 2–3 HOURS

COOKING TIME 20 MINUTES

INGREDIENTS

400 g / 14 oz / 2 ⅔ cups strong white bread
    flour, plus extra for dusting

½ tsp easy-blend dried yeast

1 tbsp caster (superfine) sugar

1 tsp fine sea salt

1 tbsp olive oil

METHOD

- Mix together the flour, yeast, sugar and salt. Stir the oil into 280 ml / 10 fl. oz / 1 ⅛ cups of warm water then stir it into the dry ingredients.

- Knead the mixture on a lightly oiled surface for 10 minutes or until smooth and elastic. Leave the dough to rest, covered with oiled cling film, for 1–2 hours or until doubled in size.

- Shape the dough into 6 torpedo-shaped rolls and transfer to a greased baking tray, then cover with oiled cling film and leave to prove for 1 hour or until doubled in size.

- Preheat the oven to 220°C (200°C fan) / 425F / gas 7.

- Dust the rolls with a little flour and slash the top of each one diagonally with a sharp knife. Transfer the tray to the top shelf of the oven.

- Bake for 20 minutes or until the rolls sound hollow when you tap them underneath. Transfer to a wire rack and leave to cool completely before serving.

TOP TIP

Serve these rolls at your next barbecue — perfect filled with sausages and coleslaw.

Walnut and Raisin Bread

MAKES 1 LOAF

PREPARATION TIME 2 HOURS 30 MINUTES

COOKING TIME 35 MINUTES

INGREDIENTS

400 g / 14 oz / 2 ⅔ cups strong white bread
    flour, plus extra for dusting

1 tsp easy-blend dried yeast

4 tbsp light brown sugar

1 tsp fine sea salt

100 g / 3 ½ oz / ¾ cup walnuts, chopped

100 g / 3 ½ oz / ½ cup raisins

2 tbsp butter, melted

2 tbsp sugar nibs

METHOD

- Mix together the flour, yeast, sugar, salt, walnuts and raisins. Stir the butter into 280 ml / 10 fl. oz / 1 ⅛ cups of warm water. Stir the liquid into the dry ingredients then knead on a lightly oiled surface for 10 minutes or until the dough is smooth and elastic.

- Leave the dough to rest, covered with oiled cling film, for 1–2 hours or until doubled in size.

- Knead the dough for 2 more minutes, then shape it into a long loaf. Transfer the loaf to a greased baking tray and cover again with oiled cling film. Leave to prove for 1 hour or until doubled in size.

- Meanwhile, preheat the oven to 220°C (200°C fan) / 425F / gas 7.

- When the dough has risen, sprinkle the top with sugar nibs. Transfer the tray to the top shelf of the oven. Bake for 35 minutes or until the loaf sounds hollow when tapped.

TOP TIP
Try serving this bread with a good mature Cheddar and pickled walnuts.

Chocolate and Dried Strawberry Bread

MAKES 2 LOAVES

PREPARATION TIME 2 HOURS 30 MINUTES

COOKING TIME 35 MINUTES

INGREDIENTS

400 g / 14 oz / 2 ⅔ cups strong white bread
flour, plus extra for dusting

1 tsp easy-blend dried yeast

4 tbsp light brown sugar

1 tsp fine sea salt

50 g / 1 ¾ oz / ½ cup unsweetened
cocoa powder

100 g / 3 ½ oz / ½ cup dried strawberries

2 tbsp butter, melted

METHOD

- Mix together the flour, yeast, sugar, salt, cocoa and strawberries. Stir the butter into 280 ml / 10 fl. oz / 1 ⅛ cups of warm water. Stir the liquid into the dry ingredients then knead on a lightly oiled surface for 10 minutes or until the dough is smooth and elastic.

- Leave the dough to rest, covered with oiled cling film, for 1–2 hours or until doubled in size.

- Knead the dough for 2 more minutes, then shape it into 2 loaves. Transfer the loaves to a greased baking tray and cover with oiled cling film. Leave to prove for 1 hour or until doubled in size.

- Meanwhile, preheat the oven to 220°C (200°C fan) / 425F / gas 7.

- Transfer the tray to the top shelf of the oven. Bake for 35 minutes or until the loaves sound hollow when tapped. Leave to cool completely on a wire rack.

TOP TIP

Sweet bread makes a great 'afternoon tea' snack!

169

Granary Bread

MAKES 1 LOAF

PREPARATION TIME 2 HOURS 30 MINUTES

COOKING TIME 35 MINUTES

INGREDIENTS

200 g / 7 oz / 1 ⅓ cups malted granary flour

200 g / 7 oz / 1 ⅓ cups strong white bread
    flour, plus extra for dusting

½ tsp easy-blend dried yeast

2 tbsp caster (superfine) sugar

1 tsp fine sea salt

1 tbsp olive oil

METHOD

- Mix together the flours, yeast, sugar and salt. Stir the oil into 280 ml / 10 fl. oz / 1 ⅛ cups of warm water then stir it into the dry ingredients.

- Knead the mixture on a lightly oiled surface with your hands for 10 minutes or until smooth and elastic. Leave the dough to rest in a lightly oiled bowl, covered with oiled cling film, for 1–2 hours or until doubled in size.

- Knead it for 2 more minutes then roll it into a fat sausage. Turn it 90° and roll it tightly the other way then tuck the ends under and transfer the dough to a lined baking tray, keeping the seam underneath. Cover with oiled cling film. Leave to prove for 1 hour or until doubled in size.

- Meanwhile, preheat the oven to 220°C (200°C fan) / 425F / gas 7.

- Transfer the tray to the top shelf of the oven. Bake for 35 minutes or until the loaf sounds hollow when you tap it underneath. Transfer to a wire rack and leave to cool completely before slicing.

TOP TIP

This bread makes excellent cheese on toast.

Onion and Poppy Seed Bread

MAKES 1

PREPARATION TIME 2 HOURS 30 MINUTES

COOKING TIME 35 MINUTES

INGREDIENTS

400 g / 14 oz / 2 ⅔ cups strong white bread
    flour, plus extra for dusting

½ tsp easy blend dried yeast

1 tbsp caster (superfine) sugar

1 tsp fine sea salt

1 tbsp olive oil

1 onion, chopped

1 tbsp poppy seeds

METHOD

- Mix together the flour, yeast, sugar and salt. Stir the oil into 280 ml / 10 fl. oz / 1 ⅛ cups of warm water and stir into the dry ingredients.

- Knead the mixture on a lightly oiled surface for 10 minutes or until the dough is smooth and elastic. Leave the dough to rest in a lightly oiled bowl, covered with oiled cling film, for 1–2 hours or until doubled in size.

- Sprinkle the onion over the bread, then knead it in until evenly mixed. Shape the bread into a round loaf and transfer to a greased baking tray. Cover the dough loosely with oiled cling film and leave to prove for 45 minutes.

- Preheat the oven to 220°C (200°C fan) / 430F / gas 7.

- Sprinkle the loaf with poppy seeds. Transfer the tray to the top shelf of the oven. Bake for 35 minutes or until the underneath sounds hollow when tapped. Leave to cool completely on a wire rack before slicing.

TOP TIP

Try serving the bread as an accompaniment to tomato soup.

Rye Cob Loaf

MAKES 1 LOAF
PREPARATION TIME 2 HOURS 30 MINUTES
COOKING TIME 40 MINUTES

INGREDIENTS

400 g / 14 oz / 2 ⅔ cups rye flour, plus extra
    for dusting
1 tsp easy-blend dried yeast
1 tbsp treacle
1 tbsp malt extract
1 tsp fine sea salt
1 tbsp olive oil

METHOD

- Mix together the flour, yeast, treacle, malt extract and salt. Stir the oil into 280 ml / 10 fl. oz / 1 ⅛ cups of warm water. Stir the liquid into the dry ingredients then knead on a lightly oiled surface for 10 minutes or until the dough is smooth and elastic.

- Leave the dough to rest, covered with oiled cling film, for 1–2 hours or until doubled in size. Knead the dough for 2 more minutes, then shape it into a round loaf. Transfer the loaf to a greased baking tray and cover again with oiled cling film. Leave to prove for 1 hour or until doubled in size.

- Meanwhile, preheat the oven to 220°C (200°C fan) / 430F / gas 7.

- Dust the top of the loaf with flour. Transfer the tray to the top shelf of the oven.

- Bake for 40 minutes or until the loaf sounds hollow when tapped. Transfer the bread to a wire rack and leave to cool completely.

TOP TIP

This bread is delicious served with roll mops and slices of apple.

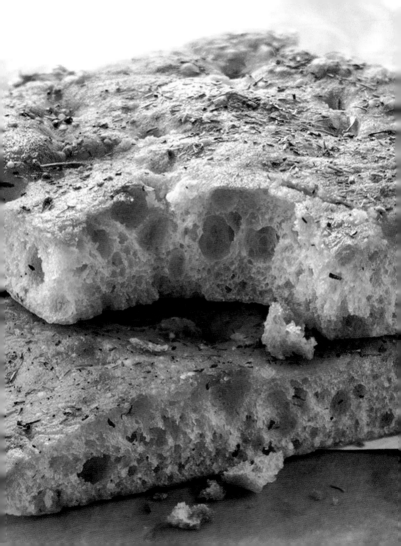

Rosemary Focaccia

MAKES 1

PREPARATION TIME 2 HOURS 30 MINUTES

COOKING TIME 25 MINUTES

INGREDIENTS

300 g / 10 ½ oz / 2 cups strong white
    bread flour

½ tsp easy-blend dried yeast

1 tsp fine sea salt

2 tbsp olive oil

TO FINISH

50 ml / 1 ¾ fl. oz / ¼ cup olive oil

50 ml / 1 ¾ fl. oz / ¼ cup warm water

½ tsp fine sea salt

1 tsp dried rosemary

METHOD

- Mix together the flour, yeast and salt. Stir the oil into 280 ml / 10 fl. oz / 1 ⅛ cups of warm water then stir it into the dry ingredients.

- Knead the mixture on a lightly oiled surface for 10 minutes or until smooth and elastic.

- Leave the dough to rest, covered with oiled cling film, for 1–2 hours or until doubled in size.

- Oil a rectangular cake tin then stretch out the dough to cover the base.

- Cover the focaccia with oiled cling film and leave to prove for 1 hour or until doubled in size.

- Preheat the oven to 220°C (200°C fan) / 430F / gas 7.

- Put the oil, water and salt in a jam jar and shake well to emulsify.

- Pour it all over the dough then sprinkle with the rosemary.

- Bake on the top shelf of the oven for 25 minutes or until the top is golden and the base is cooked through.

- Leave to cool on a wire rack before cutting into squares.

TOP TIP

Serve the focaccia with mixed charcuterie or antipasti.

Desserts

Summer Berry Pavlovas

SERVES 6
PREPARATION TIME 30 MINUTES
COOKING TIME 1 HOUR

INGREDIENTS

4 large egg whites

110 g / 4 oz / 1 cup caster (superfine) sugar

300 g / 10 ½ oz / 2 cups mixed summer berries

4 tbsp crème de cassis

300 ml / 10 ½ fl. oz / 1 ¼ cups double (heavy) cream

icing (confectioners') sugar for dusting

METHOD

- Preheat the oven to 140°C (120°C fan) / 275F / gas 1 and oil and line a large baking tray with greaseproof paper.

- Whisk the egg whites until stiff, then gradually whisk in half the sugar until the mixture is very shiny. Fold in the remaining sugar then spoon the mixture into 6 mounds on the prepared baking tray.

- Transfer the tray to the oven and bake for 1 hour, then turn off the heat and leave them to cool completely in the oven.

- While the meringues are cooking, mix the berries with the crème de cassis and leave to macerate for 1 hour 30 minutes.

- When you're ready to serve, whip the cream until it just holds its shape and spoon it on top of the meringues. Spoon over the berries and serve immediately.

TOP TIP
Try flavouring the meringues with 1 tsp of ground cinnamon.

Apple and Blackberry Crumbles

MAKES 6

PREPARATION TIME 10 MINUTES

COOKING TIME 25 MINUTES

INGREDIENTS

2 apples, peeled, cored and diced

150 g / 5 ½ oz / 1 cup blackberries

4 tbsp caster (superfine) sugar

75 g / 2 ½ oz / ⅓ cup butter

50 g / 1 ¾ oz / ⅓ cup plain (all purpose) flour

25 g / 1 oz / ¼ cup ground almonds

40 g / 1 ½ oz / ¼ cup light brown sugar

METHOD

- Preheat the oven to 180°C (160°C fan) / 350F / gas 4.

- Toss the apples and blackberries with the caster sugar and divide between 6 mini pudding basins.

- Rub the butter into the flour and stir in the ground almonds and brown sugar. Sprinkle it over the fruit, then bake for 25 minutes or until the tops are golden brown.

TOP TIP

Try using pears instead of apples.

Raspberry Fool

SERVES 4

PREPARATION TIME 15 MINUTES

INGREDIENTS

150 g / 5 ½ oz / 1 cup raspberries

50 g / 1 ¾ oz / ½ cup icing (confectioners')
    sugar

1 tsp vanilla extract

600 ml / 1 pint / 2 ½ cups double (heavy)
    cream

METHOD

- Reserve 4 raspberries for decoration and press the rest through a sieve. Add the icing sugar and vanilla and stir to dissolve.

- Whip the cream until it just holds its shape, then spoon a third of it into a piping bag fitted with a large star nozzle and set aside. Fold two thirds of the raspberry purée into the rest of the cream and divide between 4 glasses.

- Spoon the rest of the raspberry puree on top, then pipe on the reserved cream. Top each fool with a raspberry and serve.

TOP TIP
Stir a handful of white chocolate chips through the fool for a texture contrast.

Fig Crumble

SERVES 4
PREPARATION TIME 10 MINUTES
COOKING TIME 30 MINUTES

INGREDIENTS

8 fresh figs, quartered
1 lime, juiced
75 g / 2 ½ oz / ⅓ cup butter
50 g / 1 ¾ oz / ⅓ cup plain (all purpose) flour
25 g / 1 oz / ¼ cup ground almonds
40 g / 1 ½ oz / ¼ cup caster (superfine) sugar

METHOD

- Preheat the oven to 180°C (160°C fan) / 350F / gas 4.

- Arrange the figs in a baking dish and drizzle with lime juice.

- Rub the butter into the flour and stir in the ground almonds and sugar. Take a handful of the topping and squeeze it into a clump, then crumble it over the fruit.

- Repeat with the rest of the crumble mixture then bake for 30 minutes or until the topping is golden brown.

TOP TIP
Spice up the crumble topping with 1 tsp of ground mixed spice.

Cherry and Pistachio Verrines

MAKES 6

PREPARATION TIME 5 MINUTES

COOKING TIME 8 MINUTES

INGREDIENTS

300 g / 10 ½ oz / 2 cups cherries, stoned

3 tbsp kirsch

250 g / 9 oz / 2 cups amaretti biscuits,
    crumbled

3 tbsp pistachio nuts, chopped

METHOD

- Put the cherries and kirsch in a small saucepan then cover and poach for 8 minutes.

- Leave the cherries to cool to room temperature, then stir in most of the crumbled amaretti biscuits and divide between 6 glasses.

- Sprinkle the tops with pistachio nuts and the remaining amaretti biscuits before serving.

TOP TIP
Try replacing the amaretti biscuits with ginger cake for a spicy alternative.

Madeira Cake with Summer Berries

SERVES 8

PREPARATION TIME 10 MINUTES

COOKING TIME 55 MINUTES

INGREDIENTS

200 g / 7 oz / 1 ⅓ cups self-raising flour, sifted

50 g / 1 ¾ oz / ½ cup ground almonds

175 g / 6 oz / ¾ cup caster (superfine) sugar

175 g / 6 oz / ¾ cup butter, softened

3 large eggs

1 lemon, zest finely grated

150 g / 5 ½ oz / 1 cup mixed summer berries

icing (confectioners') sugar for sprinkling

METHOD

- Preheat the oven to 160°C (140°C fan) / 325F / gas 3 and line a 23 cm (9 in) round cake tin with greaseproof paper.

- Combine the flour, ground almonds, sugar, butter, eggs and lemon zest in a bowl and whisk together for 2 minutes or until smooth.

- Scrape the mixture into the tin and level the top then bake for 55 minutes or until a skewer inserted in the centre comes out clean.

- Transfer to a wire rack and leave to cool completely. Pile the berries on top of the cake and dust lightly with icing sugar before serving.

TOP TIP

Stir a handful of white chocolate chips through the cake mixture before baking.

Apple and Sultana Pie

SERVES 8
PREPARATION TIME 50 MINUTES
COOKING TIME 45 MINUTES

INGREDIENTS

1 kg / 2 lb 3 oz / 5 cups Bramley apples
125 g / 4 oz / ½ cup caster (superfine) sugar
2 tbsp plain (all purpose) flour
1 tsp ground cinnamon
75 g / 2 ½ oz / ⅓ cup sultanas

FOR THE PASTRY

200 g / 7 oz / 1 ⅓ cups plain (all purpose)
   flour
200 g / 7 oz / 1 ⅓ cups wholemeal flour
2 tbsp light brown sugar
200 g / 7 oz / ¾ cup butter, cubed
icing (confectioners') sugar for dusting

METHOD

- First make the pastry. Mix the plain flour, wholemeal flour and sugar together, then rub in the butter until it resembles fine breadcrumbs. Add just enough cold water to bring the mixture together into a pliable dough, then wrap in cling film and chill for 30 minutes.

- Preheat the oven to 190°C (170°C fan) / 375F / gas 5.

- Peel, core and quarter the apples, then slice them thinly and blot away any excess moisture with kitchen paper.

- Mix the sugar, flour, cinnamon and sultanas together in a bowl then toss with the apples.

- Set a third of the pastry aside then roll out the rest on a lightly floured surface and use it to line a deep pie tin. Pack the apple mixture in tightly.

- Roll out the reserved pastry, then roll a lattice cutter over the top. Gently ease the pastry apart to show the holes, then transfer it to the top of the pie and secure with a dab of water. Trim away any excess pastry.

- Bake the pie for 45 minutes or until the apples are tender in the centre and the pastry is crisp underneath. Serve dusted with icing sugar.

TOP TIP
Try stirring grated Cheddar into the pastry before adding the water.

DESSERTS

Treacle, Apple and Ginger Sponge Pudding

SERVES 6
PREPARATION TIME 15 MINUTES
COOKING TIME 25 MINUTES

INGREDIENTS

110 g / 4 oz / ⅔ cup self-raising flour, sifted
110 g / 4 oz / ⅓ cup dark muscovado sugar
110 g / 4 oz / ½ cup butter, softened
2 large eggs
2 tsp ground ginger
2 Bramley apples, peeled, cored and chopped
4 tbsp treacle
custard or double (heavy) cream to serve

METHOD

- Preheat the oven to 190°C (170°C fan) / 375F / gas 5 and line a small roasting tin with greaseproof paper.

- Combine the flour, sugar, butter, eggs and spices in a bowl and whisk together for 2 minutes or until smooth.

- Fold in the apple then scrape the mixture into the prepared tin and ripple through the treacle.

- Transfer the tin to the oven and bake for 25 minutes or until a skewer inserted into the centre comes out clean. Serve warm with custard or double cream.

TOP TIP
This recipe also works really well with pears instead of apples.

Raspberry and Vanilla Whoopee Pies

MAKES 18

PREPARATION TIME 35 MINUTES

COOKING TIME 10 MINUTES

INGREDIENTS

55 g / 2 oz / ⅓ cup self-raising flour, sifted

2 tsp baking powder

55 g / 2 oz / ½ cup ground almonds

110 g / 4 oz / ½ cup caster (superfine) sugar

110 g / 4 oz / ½ cup butter, softened

2 large eggs

2 tbsp raspberry syrup

TO DECORATE

100 g / 3 ½ oz / ½ cup butter, softened

400 g / 14 oz / 4 cups icing (confectioners')
   sugar

1 tsp vanilla extract

1 tbsp raspberry syrup

METHOD

- Preheat the oven to 190°C (170°C fan) / 375F / gas 5 and line 2 large baking trays with non-stick baking mats.

- Combine the flour, baking powder, ground almonds, sugar, butter, eggs and raspberry syrup in a bowl and whisk together for 2 minutes or until smooth.

- Spoon the mixture into a piping bag fitted with a large plain nozzle and pipe 18 walnut-sized domes onto each tray.

- Transfer the trays to the oven and bake for 10 minutes. The mixture should spread a little whilst cooking and the cakes will be ready when springy to the touch. Leave the cakes to cool on the tray.

- To make the buttercream, beat the butter until smooth, then beat in half of the icing sugar and the vanilla extract. Use the buttercream to sandwich the cakes together in pairs.

- Stir the raspberry syrup into the rest of the icing sugar, then use it to ice the top of the whoopee pies.

TOP TIP

The raspberry syrup can be replaced with blueberry syrup.

DESSERTS

Easy Fruit Tarts

MAKES 4

PREPARATION TIME 20 MINUTES

COOKING TIME 15 MINUTES

INGREDIENTS

400 g / 14 oz / 2 cups ready-to-roll puff pastry

your choice of fruit (apples, pears and plums
        work well)

3 tbsp icing (confectioners') sugar

1 tsp ground cinnamon

METHOD

- Preheat the oven to 220°C (200°C fan) / 425F / gas 7.

- Roll out the pastry into a rectangle on a lightly floured surface and cut into 4 rectangles or rounds. Transfer the pastry shapes to a non-stick baking tray.

- Remove the core or stones from the fruit and cut into thin slices, then arrange the fruit on top of the pastry. Mix the icing sugar and cinnamon together, then dust it liberally over the tarts.

- Transfer the baking tray to the oven and bake for 15 minutes or until the pastry is cooked through underneath and golden brown on top.

TOP TIP
Add a thin layer of marzipan between the pastry and the fruit.

Rose Water Meringues

MAKES 16

PREPARATION TIME 20 MINUTES

COOKING TIME 1 HOUR

INGREDIENTS

4 large egg whites

1 tbsp rose water

a few drops of pink food dye

110 g / 4 oz / 1 cup caster (superfine) sugar

METHOD

- Preheat the oven to 140°C (120°C fan) / 275F / gas 1 and oil and line a large baking tray with greaseproof paper.

- Whisk the egg whites until stiff with the rose water and food dye, then gradually whisk in half the caster sugar until the mixture is very shiny. Fold in the remaining caster sugar with a large metal spoon, being careful to retain as much air as possible.

- Spoon the meringue into a piping bag fitted with a large plain nozzle and pipe 16 swirls onto the baking tray.

- Transfer the tray to the oven and bake for 1 hour. Turn off the oven and leave the meringues to cool slowly inside before serving.

TOP TIP

These meringues are also delicious flavoured with orange-flower water.

Apple Cake

SERVES 8
PREPARATION TIME 15 MINUTES
COOKING TIME 55 MINUTES

INGREDIENTS

225 g / 8 oz / 1 ½ cups self raising flour
1 tsp ground cinnamon
100 g / 3 ½ oz / ½ cup butter, cubed
100 g / 3 ½ oz / ½ cup caster (superfine) sugar
1 large egg
75 ml / 2 ½ fl. oz / ⅓ cup whole milk
2 apples, peeled, cored and thinly sliced
extra caster (superfine) sugar for sprinkling
double (heavy) cream for pouring

METHOD

- Preheat the oven to 180°C (160°C fan) / 350F / gas 4 and line a 23 cm (9 in) round cake tin with non-stick baking paper.

- Sieve the flour and cinnamon into a mixing bowl, then rub in the butter until it resembles fine breadcrumbs and stir in the sugar. Lightly beat the egg with the milk and stir it into the dry ingredients until just combined.

- Fold in the apple and scrape the mixture into the tin then bake for 55 minutes or until a skewer inserted in the centre comes out clean.

- Transfer the cake to a wire rack and leave to cool completely then sprinkle with caster sugar and serve with double cream.

TOP TIP
Try making this cake with plums too when they're in season.

Pear and Blackcurrant Verrines

MAKES 8
PREPARATION TIME 15 MINUTES
COOKING TIME 20 MINUTES

INGREDIENTS

3 ripe pears, peeled, cored and chopped
150 g / 5 ½ oz / 1 cup blackcurrants
50 g / 1 ¾ oz / ¼ cup caster (superfine) sugar
300 ml / 10 ½ fl. oz / 1 ¼ cups double
    (heavy) cream
1 tsp vanilla extract
3 tbsp icing (confectioners') sugar
16 amaretti biscuits, crumbled

METHOD

- Put the pears in a saucepan then cover and cook over a medium heat for 10 minutes or until they are softly poached in their own juices. Puree until smooth, then leave to cool completely.

- Meanwhile, put the blackcurrants in a small saucepan with the sugar. Cover the pan and cook over a low heat for 10 minutes or until the blackcurrants have burst and softened. Taste the blackcurrants and add more sugar if necessary. Leave to cool.

- Whip the cream with the vanilla and icing sugar until it just holds its shape, then fold in the pear puree.

- Divide the pear cream between 8 glasses and top with the blackcurrants. Sprinkle over the amaretti biscuits and serve immediately.

TOP TIP
Try replacing the pears with cooking apples.

Carrot and Walnut Tray Bake

SERVES 10

PREPARATION TIME 25 MINUTES

COOKING TIME 40 MINUTES

INGREDIENTS

175 g / 6 oz / 1 cup soft light brown sugar

2 large eggs

150 ml / 5 fl. oz / ⅔ cup sunflower oil

175 g / 6 oz / 1 ¼ cups plain (all purpose) flour

3 tsp baking powder

2 tsp ground cinnamon

1 orange, zest finely grated

200 g / 7 oz / 1 ⅔ cups carrots, washed and coarsely grated

100 g / 3 ½ oz / ¾ cup walnuts, chopped

FOR THE ICING

110 g / 4 oz / ½ cup cream cheese

55 g / 2 oz / ¼ cup butter, softened

110 g / 4 oz / 1 cup icing (confectioners') sugar

1 tsp vanilla extract

2 tbsp walnuts, finely chopped

METHOD

- Preheat the oven to 190°C (170°C fan) / 375F / gas 5 and line a 20 cm x 15 cm (8 in x 6 in) cake tin with greaseproof paper.

- Whisk the sugar, eggs and oil together for 3 minutes until thick. Fold in the flour, baking powder and cinnamon, followed by the orange zest, carrots and walnuts.

- Scrape the mixture into the tin and bake for 40 minutes or until a skewer inserted in the centre comes out clean. Transfer the cake to a wire rack and leave to cool completely.

- To make the icing, beat the cream cheese and butter together with a wooden spoon until light and fluffy then beat in the icing sugar a quarter at a time. Add the vanilla extract then use a whisk to whip the mixture for 2 minutes or until smooth and light.

- Spread the icing over the cake and sprinkle with walnuts before cutting into 10 bars.

TOP TIP

Try stirring a handful of sultanas into the cake mixture before baking.

Almond Tea Cake

SERVES 8
PREPARATION TIME 25 MINUTES
COOKING TIME 55 MINUTES

INGREDIENTS

225 g / 8 oz / 1 ½ cups self-raising flour

1 tsp mixed spice

100 g / 3 ½ oz / ½ cup butter, cubed

100 g / 3 ½ oz / ½ cup caster (superfine) sugar

1 large egg

75 ml / 2 ½ fl. oz / ⅓ cup cold milky tea

100 g / 3 ½ oz / ⅔ cup currants

150 g / 5 ½ oz / ½ cup golden marzipan, thinly sliced

50 g / 1 ¾ oz / ⅔ cup flaked (slivered) almonds

TO GLAZE

2 tbsp butter

3 tbsp runny honey

METHOD

- Preheat the oven to 180°C (160°C fan) / 350F / gas 4 and line a 23 cm (9 in) cake tin with greaseproof paper.

- Sieve the flour and spice into a mixing bowl then rub in the butter until it resembles fine breadcrumbs. Stir in the sugar.

- Lightly beat the egg with the tea and stir it into the dry ingredients until just combined then fold in the currants and marzipan.

- Scrape the mixture into the tin and scatter over the almonds. Bake for 55 minutes or until a skewer inserted in the centre comes out clean.

- To make the glaze, melt the butter and honey together in a saucepan. When the cake has cooled, brush the mixture over the top, then cut into slices and serve.

TOP TIP

Stir a handful of halved glace cherries into the cake mixture before baking.

Chocolate Sponge Cake

SERVES 8
PREPARATION TIME 20 MINUTES
COOKING TIME 35 MINUTES

INGREDIENTS

175 g / 6 oz / 1 ¼ cups self-raising flour
175 g / 6 oz / ¾ cup caster (superfine) sugar
175 g / 6 oz / ¾ cup butter, softened
3 large eggs
1 tsp baking powder
3 tbsp unsweetened cocoa powder
raspberries to serve
icing (confectioners') sugar for dusting

METHOD

- Preheat the oven to 180°C (160°C fan) / 350F / gas 4 and grease and line a 23 cm (9 in) round loose-bottomed cake tin.

- Put the flour, sugar, butter, eggs, baking powder and cocoa in a large mixing bowl and whisk with an electric whisk for 4 minutes or until pale and well whipped.

- Scrape the mixture into the tin and level the top with a spatula. Bake for 35 minutes or until a toothpick inserted in the centre comes out clean. Transfer the cake to a wire rack and leave to cool completely.

- Arrange the raspberries on top of the cake and dust lightly with icing sugar.

TOP TIP
Top the cake with chocolate spread for a quick and easy icing.

Cherry and Marzipan Pies

MAKES 4
PREPARATION TIME 15 MINUTES
COOKING TIME 20 MINUTES

INGREDIENTS

400 g / 14 oz / 2 cups ready-to-roll sweet
    dessert pastry
150 g / 5 ½ oz / ½ cup marzipan, thinly sliced
200 g / 7 oz / 1 ⅓ cups black cherries, stoned
1 egg, beaten
1 tbsp granulated sugar

METHOD

- Preheat the oven to 200°C (180°C fan) / 400F / gas 6.

- Divide the pastry into 4 pieces and roll each piece out into a circle. Arrange a quarter of the marzipan slices and cherries in the centre of each one, then fold up and crimp the sides.

- Transfer the pies to a greased baking tray, then brush the pastry with egg and sprinkle with sugar. Bake the pies for 20 minutes or until the pastry is crisp underneath.

TOP TIP
Try using blueberries in place of the cherries.

Chocolate Bundt Cake

SERVES 8
PREPARATION TIME 25 MINUTES
COOKING TIME 45 MINUTES

INGREDIENTS

225 g / 8 oz / 1 cup butter, softened
225 g / 8 oz / 1 cup caster (superfine) sugar
4 large eggs, beaten
125 g / 4 ½ oz / ¾ cup self-raising flour
100 g / 3 ½ oz / 1 cup ground almonds
3 tbsp unsweetened cocoa powder

TO FINISH

100 g / 3 ½ oz / ¾ cup dark chocolate
    (minimum 60 % cocoa solids), chopped
28 g / 1 oz butter
2 tbsp golden syrup

METHOD

- Preheat the oven to 180°C (160°C fan) / 355F / gas 4 and butter a bundt tin.

- Cream the butter and sugar together until well whipped then gradually whisk in the eggs, beating well after each addition.

- Fold in the flour, ground almonds and cocoa then scrape the mixture into the tin.

- Bake the cake for 45 minutes or until a skewer inserted in the centre comes out clean. Turn the cake out onto a wire rack and leave to cool completely.

- Melt the chocolate, butter and syrup together over a low heat, stirring regularly, then spoon it over the cake.

TOP TIP
Substitute the dark chocolate for white chocolate for the drizzle.

Almond and Butterscotch Semifreddo

SERVES 6
PREPARATION TIME 1 HOUR
FREEZING TIME 6 HOURS

INGREDIENTS

2 large eggs, separated
100 g / 3 ½ oz / 1 cup icing (confectioners') sugar
600 ml / 1 pint / 2 ½ cups double (heavy) cream
3 tbsp Amaretto liqueur
50 g / 1 ¾ oz / ½ cup flaked (slivered) almonds

FOR THE BUTTERSCOTCH SAUCE

85 g / 3 oz / ½ cup butter
85 ml / 3 fl. oz / ⅓ cup double (heavy) cream
85 g / 3 oz / ¼ cup golden syrup
85 g / 3 oz / ½ cup dark brown sugar

METHOD

- Whisk the egg whites in a very clean bowl until stiff, then whisk in half of the icing sugar.

- Whisk the egg yolks with the rest of the icing sugar in a separate bowl for 4 minutes or until very thick.

- Whip the cream with the Amaretto in a third bowl until it holds its shape. Fold the egg yolk mixture into the cream, then fold in the egg whites.

- Line a small loaf tin with cling film, then pour in the cream mixture and level the top. Freeze for 6 hours or preferably overnight.

- To make the butterscotch sauce, stir the butter, cream, syrup and sugar together over a low heat until the butter melts and the sugar dissolves. Increase the heat and simmer for 2 minutes or until thick and smooth. Leave to cool to room temperature.

- Remove the semifreddo from the freezer 45 minutes before serving. Unmould it onto a serving plate and scatter over the almonds, then drizzle with the butterscotch sauce. Cut into 6 wedges and serve immediately.

TOP TIP
Try replacing the almonds with slivered pistachios.

Blackcurrant Cheesecakes

MAKES 6
PREPARATION TIME 25 MINUTES
COOKING TIME 40 MINUTES
CHILLING TIME 2 HOURS

INGREDIENTS

200 g / 7 oz / 1 cup digestive biscuits, crushed
50 g / 1 ¾ oz / ¼ cup butter, melted
600 g / 1 lb 5 oz / 2 ¾ cups cream cheese
150 ml / 5 fl. oz / ⅔ cup soured cream
175 g / 6 oz / ¾ cup caster (superfine) sugar
2 large eggs, plus 1 egg yolk
2 tbsp plain (all purpose) flour
1 vanilla pod, split and seeds extracted

FOR THE BLACKCURRANT TOPPING

150 g / 5 ½ oz / 1 cup blackcurrants
50 g / 1 ¾ oz / ¼ cup caster (superfine) sugar

METHOD

- Preheat the oven to 180°C (160°C fan) / 350F / gas 4 and grease 6 individual ring moulds. Place the moulds on a baking tray.

- Mix the biscuit crumbs with the butter and press into an even layer in the bottom of the moulds. Bake the biscuit layer for 5 minutes or until firm.

- Whisk together the remaining cheesecake ingredients until smooth. Spoon the cheesecake mixture on top of the biscuit bases and bake for 25 minutes or until the centres are only just set. Leave to cool completely then chill for 2 hours.

- Meanwhile, put the blackcurrants in a small saucepan with the sugar. Cover the pan and cook over a low heat for 10 minutes or until the blackcurrants have burst and softened. Taste the blackcurrants and add more sugar if necessary. Leave to cool.

- When you're ready to serve, unmould the cheesecakes and spoon the blackcurrants over the top.

TOP TIP
This recipe also works well with redcurrants instead of blackcurrants.

INDEX